THE "PEAK OIL" MYTH DEBUNKED

Prof. J. C. Mirre

ISBN: 1490551042

ISBN-13: 978-1490551043

IN MEMORIAM
Dra. Magdalena M. L. Koukharsky, a friend, college and
distinguished exploration geologist. An enthusiastic and inspiring
professor of geosciences and petrology.
She passed away in Buenos Aires, Argentina, in August 2013.

Prof. J.C. Mirre

CONTENTS

THE "PEAK OIL" MYTH DEBUNKED

THERE IS PLENTY OF OIL FOR ANOTHER CENTURY

The possibilities of finding oil in California are almost nonexistent
United States Geological Survey (USGS), 1886

The possibilities of finding oil in Texas are almost nonexistent.
United States Geological Survey (USGS), 1891

There are only reserves for another 13 years
U.S. State Department, 1939

There are only reserves for another 13 years
U.S. State Department, 1951

There is nothing left to drill in North America
Texas oil tycoon T. Boone Pickens, late 1980s

FOREWORD AND A NOTICE TO HASTY READERS

In the first place, I would like to warn the reader that this book reviews a great amount of data and numbers which could bore those who do not usually have fun with subjects such as market analyses, production statistics, consumption trends or economic forecasts.

If you have never been a member of this number-jugglers club, I suggest you to jump straight to the CONCLUSIONS at the end of the book where the basic facts disclosing that we still have oil in abundance for another century are briefly and clearly exposed.

However and if, in spite of the warning, you insist in reading through all the pages, you should know that practically all the numbers, tables and diagrams are primarily based on the Annual Statistics published by BP (ex-British Petroleum) oil company, noteworthy for their regularity and continuity (allowing to contrast data on reserves, production, consumption, etc., for the last thirty years). All figures presented by BP are accepted by the great majority of energy market analysts and in fact they are fairly within the estimations offered by other institutions like the International Energy Agency, the U.S. Geological Survey or any other outstanding international organizations.

Whenever possible, abbreviations were avoided, although in some cases well known internationally contractions such as bbl for "barrels of oil" are often used. Also repeatedly used are bbl/d for "barrels per day" or bbl/year for "barrels per year", and the same for US$/bbl for "U.S. dollars per barrel".

The information contained in this book is readily available on internet, including everything that concerns to mentions of people, institutions, foundations, universities and national or international organisms. Regarding statistical data not relative to production and reserves, which are virtually always taken from the Annual Reports of BP, the source is always indicated and readily found on internet.

Anyone can obtain on internet the same information and data used to write this book, as no confidential or private information has been quoted. In some cases, phrases or data have been taken from scientific or technical magazines, which can be found in any public or university library.

This is why there is no booklist, or list of references; readers can check data or reference simply by typing the key words on any internet search engine.

The author is a geologist, and has worked in different areas of economic or applied geology for over 40 years both in Europe and in Latin America and is perfectly familiar with the technical criteria used to evaluate reserves.

However, it is not the intention of this book to make an exhaustive analysis of the volume of reserves, or to differentiate resources from reserves, or to enter into the complex jargon lately becoming standard. The reserves figures used in this work are taken from the BP statistics, which are considered as technically recoverable by using currently available techniques. On the other hand it is not worthwhile to draw too fine a distinction, as today's skills of Enhanced Oil Recovery and directional drilling are progressing so quickly that in a few years oil deposits that are currently considered unrecoverable or uneconomic will most likely be developed and put into production. Many fields deemed "exhausted" years ago are nowadays being "restore to life" and brought back to production. Of course all depending on how much is the market ready to pay for each of the obtained barrels.

Also a very special warning to readers and critics alike: figures on oil reserves, production and future production estimates given in this book DO NOT INCLUDE "SHALE OIL", with the sole exception of USA data. The USA is the only country that accounts for all volumes of oil and "condensates" resulting from the "mining" of any liquid hydrocarbons obtained from either "gas shales" or "oil shales". In fact USA is currently the only country in the world where this type of petroleum is exploited in significant volumes (about 15% of total petroleum production), since only Canada, Australia, Mexico or Poland started very recently the combined techniques of horizontal drilling and "fracking" that allow for some economic yields from "gas shale" wells.

This means basically that even WITHOUT CONSIDERING the future (and awesome) oil reserves that will be obtained from "gas shales" and "oil shales" we HAVE PLENTY OF OIL for another century.

The object of the book is to warn people against false doomsayers that are setting up a stage of future gloom. A forthcoming menace that compel us to duck and shake, becoming easy prey and submissive followers of messianic leaders, unable to appraise whatever is dictated by the established order.

The intention is to awaken consciousness, to be aware that the bottle which is being presented as half empty is really half full or even almost completely full, that the end of oil is a phantom menace far from reality.

At the beginning of the 19th century, the Luddites were attacking textile mills and spinneries in England. Those artisans were convinced that the new machinery introduced during the Industrial Revolution would allow cloth production by unqualified workers, leaving them (the craftsmen) jobless. They strongly believed that those machines would replace their handcrafts, leaving them without a livelihood and condemned to hunger and misery. The Luddites' objectives were the machines, so they set fire to, and destroyed the mills, starting a social conflict that was quickly answered by severe repression. The movement extended all over Europe, even reaching Spain, where a late repercussion in Alcoy was, curiously enough, called "the petroleum war". The main leaders soon realized that the real enemy was the industrialist and so became the first socialists or anarchists with more specific and realistic claims, while the industry continued with its' unstoppable growth and expansion.

As with the Luddites, who misidentified their objectives, today many people sympathize with "green" groups, somehow inheritors of Luddism. For these people, oil is the "bête noire" that contaminates air, soil, water and seas. But all those fearful consequences can be solved or at least attenuated, while it is entirely ludicrous to try to halt the machinery that pulls out the reserves that Mother Nature accumulated during millions of years. The oil that lights and heats our homes, that allows us to communicate at ease and transport goods all over the planet, and so many other benefits.

We depend on oil almost as much as plants do on the sun. Mineral oil will enable our access to a brilliant future of cheap energy, entering a time ahead where we humans, like plants, will enjoy the sun as our sole source of energy.

INTRODUCTION

Nobody can deny that oil will be exhausted someday, the same as natural gas or coal or peat. Different from metallic mineral resources, which will never be exhausted simply because they can be recycled, fossil fuels, once burnt and transformed into gaseous CO_2 and water vapor, cannot be used again, even using complex or expensive technology. They are finite, non-renewable resources precisely because they are fossil, i.e. dead biological matter. Peat is the only fossil fuel which is being created right in front of our eyes; it is a special coal that is produced rapidly and continuously, although it needs several centuries to be transformed into a mass that can be burnt or otherwise used.

Therefore, it is undisputed that petroleum will, sooner or later, end, or reach a point where the extracted volume will be lower that its potential demand. However, that moment will probably never be reached, as, at some point, a substitute will be found. In History, there have been several cases where a novelty saves civilization and progress from a clear, imminent danger. In fact, the invention of agriculture and livestock breeding, some 10,000 years ago, were formulas that replaced the poor and extremely tiresome gathering of scattered edible plants and the hunting of ever more scarce and distant game.

Take, for example, wood and forests. From the 13th century on, British kings and lawmakers were becoming seriously worried about the continuing decrease of forested areas in the British Isles, due to both the growing need for wood and timber for different demands (construction, furniture, shipbuilding, etc.) or as fuel, either directly as wood, or for the production of charcoal required by the growing brewing industry (brewing beer needs a large quantity of fuel to produce water vapor and the toasting of barley).

We should consider that during the Middle Ages the average European family used about two tons of wood yearly for cooking and heating. And the needs of the growing metallurgical industry were huge (e.g.: one ton of wood was needed for the smelting of 9 lbs. of copper ore).

At the end of the Middle Age, the European poor families could not afford to be buried in a wooden coffin, and were forced to hire one for the ceremony and return it after the burial. Many English and French cathedrals used imported Scandinavian timber because it was cheaper and more

7

suitable than the local supply. Most of the reconstruction of London after the "Great Fire" of London in 1666 was made from timber imported from Germany and Sweden.

The mythical "Sherwood Forest", scene of the legendary adventures of Robin Hood and his Merry Men had totally disappeared by the time of Cromwell's Republic, before the end of the 17th century.

By then, soft coal or mineral coal was frequently used instead of charcoal or wood. At first, the extraction was done by hand and limited to outcropping layers, but over time it was developed and became truly technical transforming into a powerful mining activity by the beginning of the "Industrial Revolution" of the 18th century. There are several historical studies that prove that, had it not been for coal mining, British forests would have completely disappeared at some time between 1820 and 1830. Therefore, soft coal substituted charcoal and even wood, saving the forests from disappearance.

According to the historian N.F. Cantor, all Western Europe was on the verge of disaster at the beginning of the 16th century due to the almost total woods clearance that reduced the possibilities of hunting in the forests, a fundamental activity to supplement the protein-poor diet of the lower classes. Then, thanks to coal mining and the expansion of the maize and potato crops brought from America (with a higher caloric yield per acre), the poorest fields were slowly reforested and the ecological balance salvaged.

PART A

WHAT THE ALARMITS SAY

1 - THE FIRST DOOMSAYERS

Only 15 years after oil started flowing at the famous drilling site selected by "Colonel" Edwin Drake at Titusville (Pennsylvania), that is, in 1874, the chief geologist of the Pennsylvania Geological Survey had the honor of becoming the first doomsayer of Petroleum History by stating the imminent exhaustion of the resource: according to his calculations the reserves of kerosene would only last for four years. In other words, in 1378 Americans would be condemned to return to the old whale-oil lamps for lighting.

The prediction, of course, was not fulfilled, and in a few years, petroleum-derived, kerosene-burning lamps were being lit at night all over the planet, given that it was a low-cost product and much more efficient than other fuels.

As controversial writer B. Lomborg reminds us in his book "The Skeptical Ecologist", in 1914 the U.S. Bureau of Mines (USBM) estimated that the known oil reserves would only last for another 10 years, and later, in 1939, they announced that the reserves would be exhausted in 13 years.

By the end of the century, oil went from being the fuel of the already obsolete kerosene lamps to the supply of gasoline and diesel oil suitable for the recently invented automobiles, which demanded an acceleration of the oil production to provide for the increasing number of motor vehicles in the industrial world.

World War I not only proved that gasoline allowed quicker mobilization of troops, cannons and supplies a lot more efficiently than horses, but also that when the Soviet Revolution cut off the flow of Russian petroleum from Baku (now Azerbaijan), the first great European liquid fuel crisis was born. As a consequence, the U.S.A. became the Western world's main supplier of hydrocarbons, so much so that in 1919 the USGS (United States Geological Survey) published a report stating that in the American territory there were oil reserves for only nine more years. However, the most surprising thing about that report wasn't its' grossly erroneous calculation but its total ignorance of the world-shattering discovery of a new and gigantic oilfield at Spindletop, Texas in 1901. A finding that was immediately followed by new fields that would end up making Texas the world's major oil producer for several decades.

But the expert fatalists of the USGS wouldn't give up, and in 1920 they declared that the world's petroleum reserves would never exceed the 60 billion barrels (today equivalent to two years of the world's yearly consumption). Then, in 1950, while new gigantic fields were being discovered around the world, they were compelled to make some corrections and multiplying those figures by ten. Finally, in 1995, the USGS displayed new figures gauging world reserves at two trillion barrels (2×10^{12} bbl), well above the last estimates (2012) for world reserves of 1.652 trillion barrels (1.652×10^{12} bbl).

2 - OIL WILL SOON BE EXHAUSTED!

Given that the fatalist theories of oil depletion have been announced year after year during the last century, doomsayers are facing a growing defiance to their alarms. They have shouted "Wolf!", "Wolf!" so many times that it's possible that, pretty soon, no one will listen to their alarm bells. In truth, because the wolf doesn't exist.

The only thing that is for granted is that the oil stored in the planet's sedimentary basins will be exhausted someday, since apparently oil is a non-renewable resource (though we should remember that there is an abiogenic theory for hydrocarbons which, if correct, would mean it will never dry up). But the futurologists want to show how smart they are and are always trying to give a date or a year for that end, or at least predict how many more years are left until the world reaches a quasi-catastrophic situation. That day when gas stations will close, unsupplied, or when people will queue at the pump with their rationing stamps, nostalgic of the past times of "fill'er Up". Don't forget this scenario is still in the minds of senior citizens that suffered fuel rationings during the Yom Kippur war.

All the predictions about the "coming" exhaustion of oil are based on two fundamental premises:

i - That oil is a non-renewable resource, that someday will be depleted.
When a new oil field is discovered and extraction begins, the total volume

of oil pumped up increases as more wells are drilled, while the reserves decrease. At some point during the life of the field, a "maximum" is reached, the "optimum extraction peak". From then on, the withdrawal starts to decreases until the removed volume becomes so small that pumping becomes unprofitable. This concept of profitability is fundamental, because it is strongly tied to the price of oil. For example, it could seem unbeneficial to operate a well that is producing only 10 barrels a day, which can be sold for a price of 30 US$/barrel. But there would be no hesitation in keeping up the pumping gear (with all the associated costs such as technical supervision, storage and transport of the extracted crude, security measures, separation of the water and gases that are pulled out together with the oil, etc.) if the crude price attains 100 US$/barrel. Between 1973 and 1985, many abandoned wells were re-opened in the U.S. and other countries as a result of the huge increase in oil prices. The same thing has happened in the last years since 2005, even to the point of re-drilling old wells to improve their yield. This is the case of the old oil field at Ayoluengo in Burgos, Spain, that has been re-drilled recently, rescheduling this field back to production after being idle for several years. Actually, the relationship between the exploitation of a resource and its' market price is so obvious that it almost doesn't merit an explanation, and it would be foolish to ignore it. As everyone could guess, a farmer would not bother picking his harvest of oranges if the market price wouldn't compensate the cost or the troubles, while he would quickly hire labor, packaging and transport as soon as the market price soars. Americans are well familiar to the dramatic scenes of dumping and burning of oranges depicted by John Steinbeck's *Grapes of Wrath*. A different problem could arise from a badly planned oil withdrawal that can end in a well brought to over-exploitation, as has happened at many fields in the past. As oil floats on a layer of water (usually salty), when it is pumped up forcefully, the underlying watery layer can invade the well, rendering it useless. Oil geologists and engineers customarily know how to calculate the yield of a field to avoid these technical disasters. Consequently, sometimes it is better to extract the oil by using few wells, or pulling out smaller volumes, that to try to "drain" the field, leaving a large part of the reserves buried and useless, or only recoverable by using expensive and complicated techniques of extraction.

Politicians, economists and most people believe that, in general, the normal history of oil production of a field follows a Gaussian curve: a bell-shaped curve in which the highest point, or "peak", marks the highest rate of extraction for that field's historical production. However, as we have seen, the petroleum in absorbed in a porous, deeply buried rock and its' withdrawal has a cost. This cost is related to the pumping yield of the field (it is not the same to pump up 10 bbl/d as it is to remove 100 bbl/d). This yield does not depend only on the amount of oil that remains buried, but also on the extraction technique (that's why old wells are sometimes re-drilled). As we'll see further on, there are enhanced recoveries techniques that allow more juice to be squeezed from the deposit, techniques that are improving on a daily basis. The consequence of all this is that the famous "Gaussian Bell" becomes asymmetrical, as can be seen in FIGURE 1, with a very pronounced slope in the first years at the start of the field's life, that is followed by a slow decline over the years as reserves are depleted.

ii - That the total quantity of oil stored in the buried rocks will never be extracted. In Nature, hydrocarbons are found as a more or less viscous liquid that saturates certain porous rocks. The amount of petroleum that saturates the rock will depend on the number of pores contained in the rock; the more porous, the higher the amount of liquid occupying the spaces between the mineral grains, and easier the removal of oil. But a point is always reached when the petroleum adhered to the mineral grains becomes impossible to "loosen". A comparison which helps to understand this basic concept is to compare the storing rock to a damp towel. If one squeezes the towel you can get a lot of water out of it, but you will reach a point at which, no matter how hard you squeeze, you will not get a single drop from the towel. As we will see further on, there are several methods to try to obtain the maximum quantity of oil out of the rock, techniques known as Enhanced Oil Recovery (EOR).

3 - THE HISTORICAL PRODUCTION CURVE IS NOT A GAUSSIAN BELL

The productive history of an oil field starts with the withdrawal from the first well, generally the "discovery" well. We are at the origin or base of the curve. As new wells are drilled, the volume of oil increases, going from "discovery well" to "field". Years later, the number of wells drilled on the field is dense enough to define the field's fundamental parameters: reserves and optimum extraction yield. When the "plateau" (not the "peak") of maximum production is reached, it no longer makes sense to increase the number of extraction wells drilled, as the production will remain stable. A few years later, a phase of "diminished yield" is reached, i.e. the yield per well is reduced, at which time economic analyses are undertaken to evaluate the use of an enhanced oil recovery technique (EOR), such as, for example, injecting water. With the use of EOR, not only is the decline in oil production stopped, but the yield of the field can even be increased to volumes very close to those of the past "plateau". After a time (usually several years) the oil recovery drops again. The operating company may then initiate a new phase of EOR, a.k.a. secondary or tertiary EOR, using more complex techniques such as injecting steam, or chemical emulsifiers, or CO_2 (see "Enhanced Oil Recovery techniques" ahead). This cycle of practices allow for many more years of production than those forecasted by a simple "Gaussian Bell". Nowadays there are EOR techniques that grant up to a 55% or 60% recoveries of the oil "in situ", i.e. more than half of the fluid the fills the pores of the reservoir rock (in which the extracted fluid is normally replaced by water). A theoretical example of the difference between the historical production curve of a field by the use of EOR procedures and the "Gaussian Bell" can be seen in FIGURE 1. In fact, oil production statistics for the U.S. reveal that, during 2011, 60% of the total production came from old wells beyond their "peak", some pumping less than 10 bbl/day a.k.a. "strippers". We shouldn't forget that, in the majority of the cases, it is more profitable to increase the yield of an old field than to start production in a new play. Old fields usually have a well-developed infrastructure for access, exploitation, dewatering, and transport of the extracted oil, that allow for cost savings in contrast to the expenditures demanded when starting a new field. There are also other factors, such as environmental, economic and political issues which can favor the investment in expensive cutting-edge EOR techniques at an old field rather than the hurdles resulting from the development of new ones.

FIGURE 1 – THE HISTORICAL PRODUCTION CURVE IS NOT A "GAUSSIAN BELL" CURVE

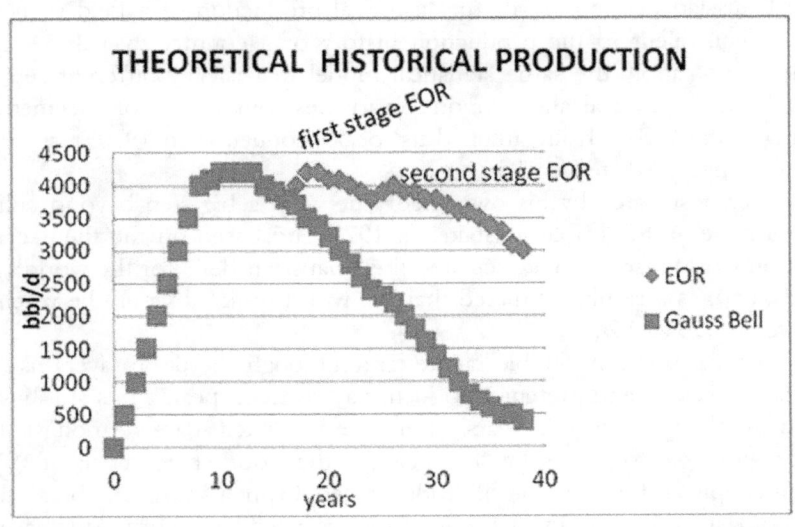

4 - KING HUBBERT'S ERROR

During the mid-1950's, petroleum geologists and engineers had enough production statistics, experience and data on oil well productivity to make a few assertions on future production and reserves depletion for most of the American oilfields. Then, in 1956, at a meeting of the American Petroleum Institute at San Antonio, Texas, the geophysicist Marion King Hubbert (1903 - 1989) ventured to add up the different Gaussian Bell distributions of historical production that showed each of the American oilfields and put together a curve comprising the past production of ALL THE NATIONS' OIL FIELDS. He then concluded that, as was the case with each of the known oilfields, the overall historical production of the Lower 48 States could be statistically considered as a Gaussian Bell distribution as is followed by each individual field. According to his theory, as new fields were discovered, the country's production would increase, and, by graphing the production against time, one would get a new GAUSSIAN BELL, whose peak would indicate the year in which maximum production was obtained, and whose total enclosed surface area would indicate the total recoverable reserves of the nation.

How is it that no new oilfield discovery would change the Bell Curve? No one knows.

Notice that K. Hubbert's theory is no longer based on the physical parameters of a single field and its' rate of production and depletion, but on the total petroleum produced over the years by a nation (take into account that until 1956, the U.S. had always been the world's major oil producer). The Gaussian distribution of the historical production of a field is by no means equivalent to the production history of a country over 100 years. You cannot apply the same statistical model to basically different sets of data both in physical and economic variables. But the theory seemed to work, as the U.S.A. really attained its' peak production in 1970, just as K. Hubbert had predicted in 1956.

However, fascinated by his own theory he went a big step beyond falling into a huge, unforgivable, mistake. In 1971, and based on the then scarce data on world reserves, he calculated the "Gaussian Bell" for the world's oil fields, and, as a result, estimated that the world peak oil would be reached between 1995 and 2000.

This time, it was a miserable failure, and although the doomsayers use all kinds of excuses and pretenses to justify a "retarded peak", this still hasn't been reached 17 or 12 years after the predicted date. Amongst the arguments used to justify the "late peak" is the world energy crisis of 1973, when supply and production of crude slowed down, a short time break that did not last for long and which was further eclipsed by the brutal increase in oil prices, which contributed to a re-launching of exploration. Similar arguments are used in the cases of the economic recessions of the '80s and '90s which reduced the demand for oil, something that had tenuous effects on the world's extraction rate, totally outshined by other events producing exactly the opposite outcomes, such as:

a)   The fall of Berlin Wall and the following dismemberment of the USSR, which led to an increase of oil and its' byproducts in the former communist countries (chiefly gasoline and diesel fuels for transport).

b)   The economic growth and industrial development of China and India, which became major oil consumers.

c)   The freeze on the construction of new nuclear power plants following the Three Mile Island and Chernobyl accidents, which forced many countries to revert to thermal power stations based on oil burning so as to keep to the planned power production.

All of these important factors not only compensate for the slight reductions seen, but should have "anticipated the peak" some years before 1995 or 2000.

5 -   THE FATALISTS MISS THE TARGET ONCE AND AGAIN

In 1995 the magazine World Oil published an article by the then prestigious geologist L.H. Ivanhoe, who predicted that the world's oil production would peak between 1996 and 2000. As in the case of C. Campbell and J. Laherrère, which we shall see further on, his stunning sentence has proved to be totally wrong: *"Those who defend the utterly unscientific concept that there are sufficient reserves are moved by political reasons. The majority of exploitable deposits of petroleum have already been found, and there will be an inevitable crisis at the beginning of the next century"*. He was so confident on his ideas that, with a group of professors and friends from the famous Colorado School of Mines, founded the M. King Hubbard Center for Petroleum Supply Studies, which had the mission of gathering and evaluating information on the world's oil reserves. The Center was publishing yearly progress on the results of its research, but stopped doing so in 2003, following the death of L.H. Ivanhoe, who didn't get to see the unpleasant evidence that his heralded maximum "peak" had not been reached in 2000 (nor in 2013). He also didn't know that, despite his astonishing phrase, many new fields were discovered after his dramatic article of 1995.

The IEA (International Energy Agency) is an organism of the OECD (Organization for Economic Co-operation and Development) or "Rich

Countries Club" (although, due to the ambiguous and hypocritical American politics, China is not included, but "rich" countries such as Greece, Slovak Republic, Portugal and Luxemburg, are). It was created in 1973 in response to the oil crisis, its' fundamental objective being to maintain a steady petroleum supply to its member countries.

The IEA announced in November 2010 that the peak in crude oil production had been reached in the year 2006! In other words, according to them, we should have had 7 years of diminishing production. Something must have gone wrong!

According to their figures, in 2006 oil production reached 68 million barrels per day (the "peak" according to them), and the other 14 million produced to make the total of 86 million bbl/d produced in 2012, should be considered as "non-conventional petroleum production" and "fluids derived from gas production (condensed gases)". A trick to validate an erroneous prediction.

This way, all the oil produced above the 68 million bbl/d mark would be, ad-infinitum, "non-conventional petroleum", as the peak had been already reached in 2006.

What a laugh!

There is no "conventional" or "non-conventional" oil. There is just petroleum stored in rocks which is extracted by different techniques and sold on the market as "petroleum", taken to the refineries to obtain its' byproducts, and that is traded internationally per barrel, independent of its source, whether it results from shales, Enhanced Recovery methods, offshore, deep-offshore or ultra-deep offshore. Distinguishing between "conventional" and "non-conventional" is just a statistical sleight-of-hand to justify wrong predictions.

Using the same doomsayers' tricks we could discriminate between "conventional agriculture" if the fields are plowed and labored like a century ago and "unconventional agriculture", if we use high-yield, hybrid seeds, fertilizers or pesticides. Or "conventional mining" if coal is extracted from an underground mine, and "non-conventional mining", when from mechanized, open-pit, mines.

But the ultimate doomsayer are a group of oddities organized into the so-called ASPO (Association for the Study of Peak Oil), founded by Colin Campbell in 2006. They declare that their predictions are not solely based on K. Hubbert's Gaussian Bell, but completed and supplemented by novel sources, although they never made clear what sort of "other data" they refer to. Anyway, their foundational objectives declare that the production maximum had already occurred in 1997, and, as that was not so, systematically retard the "peak" every year 'til their last report in 2012, in which they justify the "peak" in 2006 (having "forgotten" 1997 by using the same trick thought up by the IEA, already mentioned). Believe it or not they still maintain that world oil production will immediately fall short of consumption needs and that OPEC reserves figures are "grossly overestimated". And after all those years of deceptive wailing, they still have followers and they still get funds from governments! We'll come back to the monumental errors committed by the ASPO and Colin Campbell.

2004 ESTIMATIONS BY ASPO, in million bbl/d (real 2010 figures in parentheses):

YEAR	US-48	Europe	Russia	Near E.	Others	WORLD
2005	3.4	5.2	9.1	20	47	85
2010	2.7 (4.9)	3.6 (3.8)	8 (10.3)	20 (25)	50 (38)	84.3 (82)
2020	1.7	1.8	5.4	20	37	65.5
2050	0.4	0.3	1.5	12	30	44.3

It is also worth stressing that according to ASPO, the deep offshore oil fields would peak in **2009!!!**

The Club of Rome has the merit of being the first organizations to call attention to the future exhaustion of oil. It did so in 1968, in the first of its well-known reports on *The Limits to Growth*.
This independent organization is a mixture of scientists, significant personalities from political and economic circles, past heads-of-state and, in general, "important people". The 1972 report estimated some 20 years to reach the world's peak oil production, undoubtedly the most inappropriate of the erroneous predictions. But they weren't discouraged, and twenty years later, in 1992, a new report was published: *Beyond the Limits to Growth*, which stated that Humanity had surpassed the capacity of the planet to sustain it. Finally, in 2004 they published a fresh "imminent disaster", exultantly labeling the report as *The Limits to Growth, the 30 year Update*. The heartbreaking thing is that, 40 years after the systematic failure of all the Club of Rome's predictions, there are still scientists that support their repeated "alerts" and who, based on their "predictions", still plan world regional economies and still propose the adoption of planet-wide measures.

But there is more still. *The Hirsch Report*, also given the pompous name of *World's Maximum Petroleum Production: Impacts, Mitigation and Risk Management* resulted from an assignment by the U.S. Department of Energy (DOE) to a team of technicians led by the engineer Robert Hirsch in 2005. Actually, the report does not give a specific date or year for "peak oil" after which the world's oil production would inevitably fall; instead they propose a number of mitigation policies to overcome the "imminent" (?) oil depletion. In one of the latest versions, the 2010 one, the Hirsch Report has the audacity to indicate that the world peak oil will be reached in 2015.

Another curious character is David Straham, who declares himself to be a "reporter specialized in energy matters". In 2007 he published a book called *The Last Oil Shock* and is currently the author of the web page called: www.davidstraham.com.

One of the most intriguing sections of his web page is called *"Depletion Atlas"*. On a world map, he shows 60 countries that have reached their peak production and are, therefore, in a depletion stage.

Amongst the "countries with depleted reserves" he includes none other than Venezuela, the country with the world's highest oil reserves! According to "expert" D. Straham, Venezuela reached its peak production in 1970, producing 3,754,000 bbl/d of oil, and since then has dropped to the 2012 production of 2,725,000 bbl/d. What this gentleman forgets to mention is that Venezuela has had another two episodes of lower production after 1970: in 1985 the production dropped to only 1,744,000 bbl/d and in 1998 when the yield was 3,480,000 bbl/d, a figure not too far from the 1970 level.

What is more absurd and in totally contrary to K. Hubbert's theory is to say that a country that declares having reserves of almost 300 billion barrels, enough to supply the whole world for 10 years, is today in depletion. It is an essential contradiction in respect to K. Hubbert's theory as the area enclosed beneath the Gaussian Bell is equivalent to the URR (Ultimate Recovery Resource), that is, the total extractable oil of that country (Straham figures wouldn't reach a tenth of the official data).

An important detail about the Gaussian Bell

By definition, and by mathematics, the area enclosed by the curve and the diagram's abscissa axis, where the years of the oilfield, or country production, are indicated, from the start to the foreseeable exhaustion, is equal to the total petroleum reserves or URR (ultimate recovery resources) of that field or country. This holds both for the "bell" as well as the "Historical Production Curve" of an oilfield, as is shown in FIGURE 1.

This seems obvious, but, as we shall see further on, many fatalists believe that countries with ENORMOUS HYDROCARBON RESERVES such as VENEZUELA, are in a stage of depletion. If this were true, it would result in an impossible Gaussian, or Production Curve, as it would never enclose an area equal to the declared reserves. As we shall see further on, this example can be applied to many countries considered to be "exhausted" while they actually rank amongst the top producers and hold the biggest reserves, as is the case with Iran, Russia, Mexico, etc.

The typical historical production curves of many countries are quite different from the classical, theoretical Gaussian Bell, because they suffer continuous ups-and-downs in their productions. These oscillations are related to economic circumstances, like nationalizations, privatizations, armed conflicts (such as the case of Kuwait, Iraq and Iran), or the result of erroneous or capricious political economies, normally associated to state oil monopolies. It is an unforgivable mistake to make every phase of high production a peak and every fall in production the start of depletion.

In many cases it is only the result of the infamous interference of politicians who consider that investing in exploration does not produce votes, nor guarantee their hold on power.

6 - POLITICS IS THE KEY TO EXPLAIN SOME "DEPLETIONS"

Another illustrative example of nefarious meddling of politics (although the more correct term would be "corruption") in the petroleum industry is Mexico.

If the reader bothers to compare the drilling sites in the Gulf of Mexico (e.g.: on Wikipedia: "Offshore oil and gas in the US Gulf") he will see an enormous density of drilling points or wells' locations in the U.S. territorial waters, and next to none in Mexican waters. While the U.S. has defined 190 offshore oil fields in the Gulf by means of about 4,000 exploration wells, Mexico has hardly drilled some 600, and, if we exclude the Cantarell and the Ku-Mallob-Zaap fields in the Campeche Sound (which is not strictly speaking "Gulf of Mexico"), the total does not reach 400. To stress the point, while in the U.S. sector of the Gulf 265 wells were drilled in 2012, only 59 were spudded in Mexican waters. But even then, these figures are exceptional for the last decade of the Mexican side of the Gulf. The best discovery in those waters was the new Ayin field, where reserves of some 334 million barrels were reported, a rich field still undeveloped.

We can surely say that by at the end of 2012, the Mexican sector of the Gulf is unexplored, while the U.S. production in this region represents some 2 million bbl/day (around 30% of the total American production). The Gulf is also a very rich natural gas source, which, in part, is exported to Mexico, a net importer of natural gas from USA!

Possibly, it is hoped that when Mexican politicians will find new victims or get distracted by something else to fill their pockets and letting technicians fully develop the Gulf resources, the country might increase its production levels, maybe even surpassing it's 2004 "peak" of 3,824,000 bbl/d. Or maybe even getting to a new peak of 4 million bbl/d, to the shame of D. Straham.

Incredibly, Mr. Straham considers depleted not only countries like

Venezuela, the country holding the world biggest oil reserves, but also Iran, the world's third-ranked in oil reserves.

The ridiculous argument to include Iran amongst the countries in depletion stage is based on the comparison between the present 4,226,000 bbl/d production and the 6,064,000 bbl/d production attained in 1974. For Mr. Straham that's enough to make Iran an oil-depleted country. As in previous cases, it is an essential contradiction of K. Hubbert's theory, as the area enclosed by the Bell Curve is equivalent to the URR, so that according to Mr. Straham's learned considerations, Iran's official reserves of 137 billion barrels are erroneously gauged.

The same, silly argument is used to consider many other countries with large reserves as having passed their "peak" production, and already entered into depletion. In the case of Russia, the 1982 production of 11,594,000 bbl/d is considered the "peak", although that "peak" has been sustained for eight consecutive years, until 1990, when production fell to an average of 10 to 11 million bbl/d, followed by a slight decrease, and an immediate "rebound" back to 10 million bbl/d, a flow that has been maintained from 2006 'til today (2013). You don't have to be an expert market analyst to link Russia's drop in production between 1990 and 2006 with the social and economic consequences of the chaos that followed the disintegration of the U.S.S.R., and the painful transit from the communist, state-controlled regime to an open market economy.

The historical evolution of the legendary Baku field is a clear example of the idiocy in confusing a decline in a field production due to economic or political reasons with "a depletion stage". The Baku field had at least three historical "peaks": the first in 1901 when they reached 212,000 bbl/d a triumph for those days' practices. This was followed by a second peak of 475,000 bbl/d when the Soviet engineers updated the extraction techniques in 1940, a necessary step to enable the refueling of the *Panzer* tanks and other war vehicles that the Nazis used to invade the rest of Europe (with the exception of the U.S.S.R.). The third one was attained in 1965, at 400,000 bbl/d, thanks to the shallow-water, offshore drilling in the Caspian Sea. Nowadays, with the development of the Caspian Chirag-Azeri-Guneshli offshore deep-water field, the production is close to 1,000,000 bbl/d, although possibly still not the real peak, as more discoveries and developments are expected in the coming years.

Matthew Simmons is perhaps one of the gloomiest doomsayers who confused "the end-of-oil era" with his own death. He predicted the "World Peak", for 2009, but he died soon after, in 2010, when he was 67, enough to pass over his mistake. Of course, the strange circumstances surrounding his death (he drowned in his own bathtub), somewhat similar to the passing of Bakhtiari, another doomsayer, was at the origin of rumors and conspiracy theories rife in some circles (Mossad's black hand or similar). To make matters worse, at that time, Simmons had become the outstanding censor against BP's practices following the Macondo disaster in the Mexican Gulf. In his role as a doomster, this Mormon banker (no technical background) was one of the original promoters of the idea that Saudi Arabia authorities systematically lie in their official statement of reserves. According to Simmons' own calculations (based on "leaks by Saudi technicians"), the Ghawar mega-field was, in 2009, clearly in the "exhaustion" phase.

The Ghawar field now produces 5 million bbl/ d, approximately half of the Saudi production, the equivalent of MOST of the oil production of the U.S. Its' reserves are calculated (2012) at 71.000 million bbl, which would allow production, at today's pace, for another 39 years (until 2050). Ghawar has been producing oil since 1951, albeit at a lower rate than today. Some experts believe Ghawar reached its maximum production in 2005, while others disagree, maintaining that it still hasn't "peaked" production.

Another alarmist prediction was made by the already mentioned Ali Morteza Samsam Bakhtiari, a chemical engineer with the National Iranian Oil Company. According to the calculations he made in the year 2000, oil should have reached its maximum production in 2007. Actually, it was a cruel prediction, as 2007 was the year of his death, a fatal heart attack when he was 61 years old. Bakhtiari was part of the Oil Depletion Analysis Center together with C. Campbell, a foundation started in the U.K. by several former executives of different oil companies, and whose fundamental mission was to alert the public and politicians of the imminent depletion of petroleum resources. Bakhtiari went so far as to assure that Iran's reserves are well below the 137 billion barrels officially declared, maintaining that they don't even attain the 35 billion mark. He also argued that the Ghawar mega-field in Saudi Arabia, the world's largest oil field, was in depletion stage and reducing its production at an alarming rate.

At the beginning of 2010, a group of engineers from the University of Kuwait, coordinated by Sami Nashawi, published an article in the *Energy Fuels* magazine of the American Chemical Society. The article summarizes a new analytical technique developed by the authors called: *The Multicyclic Hubbert Prediction* which takes into account many more variables than the conventional Bell Curve established by K. Hubbert in the '50s. To summarize: the world oil peak production will take place in 2014, and later, around 2026, in the OPEC countries. They estimate that, based on production and reserves of the 47 countries considered "significant producers, or higher", there are still reserves of 1.16 trillion barrels (an amount clearly below the 1.67 trillion calculated by BP for world oil reserves in 2012).

At the present rate of production (86 million bbl/d) these reserves would indicate that there is still enough oil for the next 53 years, but this period will be shortened if we consider a yearly consumption increase of 2%.

The authors repeat Mr. Straham's mistake of including in their list of "countries in depletion stage" states like Iran, which occupies 3rd. position in world reserves, or Russia (7th position). They even consider China as depleted, when China has never stopped increasing its production since 1965, whilst at the same time keeping its reserves.

As shown in TABLE I, the Kuwaiti engineers' predictions have failed miserably in the cases of U.S.A., Canada, Russia, China and Iran. On the other hand, take notice of the impressive average increase of 10% in oil production over a 5 years lapse by China, Canada and the U.S.A. The cases of the United Kingdom, Norway and Indonesia will be analyzed further on, and, in the Mexican case, the decrease in production is undoubtedly related to the low, or null, investment in exploration and particularly their "dragging their feet" in respect to the Gulf of Mexico offshore resources.

TABLE I analyzes the data from some of the countries the Kuwaiti engineers consider being in a "depletion phase" since 2005. Their forecast is compared to the real productions for 2005, 2008, and 2012 (as thousands of bbl/d).

TABLE I

OIL PRODUCTION IN SOME COUNTRIES DEEMED "DEPLETED" BY THE KUWAITI IN 2005 (thousands of bbl/d)

COUNTRY	2005	2008	2012
USA	6895	6736	8905
CANADA	3041	3238	3741
RUSSIA	9552	9886	10643
CHINA	3627	3795	4156
IRAN*	4233	4325	3680*
MEXICO	3760	3157	2911
NORWAY	2969	2455	1619
U. KINGDOM	1809	1544	967
INDONESIA	1087	1004	918
WORLD	81485	82015	86152

*IRAN production was 4358 thousand bbl/d in 2011, before the embargo

Another famous doomsayer is Chris Skrebowski, director of the company Peak Oil Consulting, and editor of the magazine *Petroleum Review*, edited by the Energy Institute of the United Kingdom (with suspicious ties to the Shell oil company). He bases his predictions reckonings, on his own secretive program called *Global Oil Megaprojects Database*. In 2006 he used this program to calculate that the world peak oil would happen before 2011, a totally false assertion as the global oil production in 2013 has been steady increasing with no signs of fall or depletion.

We shouldn't forget Kenneth S. Deffeyes, an American geologist focused on petroleum geology, and who, in his younger years, worked together with King Hubbert in the Shell company before becoming a professor at Princeton University. He published two books: *Hubbert's Peak* in 2001 and *Beyond Oil: The view from Hubbert's Peak*, in 2005. As many others, this geologist preaches that the world oil peak has already passed, according to him, **¡in 2005!**

We should also mention David Goodstein, who is not a geoscientist, but a physicist, and lately professor at the California Institute of Technology. Currently, he is mainly involved in divulging science, making scientific language simple and attractive for children and youngsters. In his book *Out of Gas: The end of the Age of Oil*, published in 2004, he mistakenly calculates peak oil for 2010, a date from which, the world oil production should have started to fall on dismal.

TABLE II – R.C. DUNCAN'S FLAWED PREDICTION (thousand bbld)

COUNTRY	Peak Year	PEAK	REAL (2012)	RESULT
USA	1970	11,297	8,905	True?
CANADA	2007	3,297	3,741	False
MEXICO	2007	3,824	2,811	False
ARGENTINA	1998	890	664	False
BRAZIL	2008	1,899	2,149	False
U.KINGDOM	1999	2,909	967	True
IRAN	1974	6,060	3,680	False
IRAQ	1979	3,489	3,115	False
KUWAIT	1972	3,339	3,127	False
S. ARABIA	1979	10,270	11,530	False
ARGELIA	2006	2,016	1,667	False
ANGOLA	2011	1,730	1,784	False
VENEZUELA	1970	3,754	2,725	False
NORWAY	2001	3,418	1,916	False
NIGERIA	2008	2,499	2,417	False
LYBIA	1970	3,357	1,509	False
CHINA	2008	3,809	4,155	False
WORLD	2008	81,544	86,152	FALSE

Another curious character was Richard C. Duncan, the ill-fated director of the Energy and Man Institute, who produced the oddly named *Graphic-Heuristic System*, a computer program that "allowed" him to foresee in 2005 that world peak oil would be attained a year later. Before his death in 2010, he proposed his "Olduvai Theory" which, amongst other catastrophes, predicted that black-outs would start in U.S.A. early in 2008, as a result of dwindling supplies of coal and oil.

TABLE II, above, shows some of the counties doomed by R.C. Duncan indicating the year of the peak production predicted and the real current (2012) production shown as thousand barrels/day (thousand bbld).

This ominous prediction would only be the harbinger of the tremendous world chaos which would come about in 2015, when the world's population would start to decrease after having reached its peak at 7,000 million people (already surpassed and still growing today).

Like many other doomsayers, R. C. Duncan emphasized that after those gloomy days, many basic raw materials would also peak and its shortage would be the cause of a global industrial collapse.

We should not forget the predictions of the EIA (Energy Information Administration), a U.S. federal agency, which depends on the Department of Energy. Established in 1977, the EIA is dedicated to the gathering, classifying and ordering of all official and private information on energy resources, both for the U.S.A. and the rest of the world. This agency compiles yearly reports on the world energy situation, and every now and then, updates all energy issues from different countries. In their latest statements they consider that the world peak oil will be attained by 2016.

7 - CHANGE OF STRATEGY: OIL WON'T PEAK, BUT WILL BE EXPENSIVE

The truth is that the doomsayers and their "research institutes" had gone over-board: not only has world oil production not peaked, but it has actually grown year after year. The terrible, apocalyptic days of an oil production unable to meet the demand never materialized and people started to mistrust the "experts" forecasts.

But with a few tricks they are now back on the bandwagon, plucking a new argument out of their top hats: "it's not that there will not be enough oil, but it will become more and more expensive every day, pricing itself out of the common man's reach" The same old song, but with new lyrics.

The modern doomsayers are not condemning us to a freezing world without oil, but to the penalties of exorbitant prices whenever approaching a refueling gas station, no matter how hybrid might our car be. They now declare that the peak date is unimportant, since we are already facing times of shortages (?), and soon we'll get used to paying for gas more than we do for French champagne. In a few years (perhaps months), -they proclaim-, gas will be a luxury item.

As we have already stated, it is obvious that, someday, oil will run out. This is something nobody questions and we need no pointless foundations or organizations, nor some infamous oddity, to tell us what seems to be obvious for everyone.

On the other hand, the "expensive oil" line of argument has no real base, because, IN CONSTANT DOLLAR VALUE, THE PRICE OF OIL HAS HARDLY GONE UP OVER THE LAST 35 YEARS. Actually, the highest-priced crude oil period was between 1979 and 1982, with an average price of US$ 88.3, while the average price between 2007 and 2010 has been US$79.2.

The relationship between price and production/reserves will be elucidated in more detail in ANNEX IV.

Amongst the "end of cheap oil" strategists is Jean Laherrère, a French geophysicist who has worked most of his life for the French oil company Total, actively participating in the discovery of the large Algerian oil fields in 1956. After retiring in 1991, he became a follower of Peak Oil theories, writing in 1998, together with Colin Campbell the famous *Scientific American* article: *The End of Cheap Oil*. Since then, he actively participated in all matters related to petroleum depletion and in 2005 founded the French branch of the ASPO (Association for the Study of Peak Oil and Gas). In the Scientific American article he supports the idea that the world peak oil would be reached in the decade between 2000-2010. In this repeatedly quoted article by Colin Campbell and Jean Laherrère there are several "gems" of blunder, such as:

a)   *"Our analysis of the discovery and production of oil fields indicates that during the next decade (that is: 2000-2010) supply won't be able to cope with demand"* (here underlined).

That is false, at no moment between 2000 and 2012 has there been unsatisfied demand. The price oscillations in the past thirteen years are due to several factors among which: the unstoppable depreciation of the dollar, several political and economic issues (i.e.: the current bans on Iranian exports following their supposed intent to fabricate nuclear weapons, a situation very similar to the NATO attitude against Saddam's Iraq or the recent NATO intervention in Libya, or the invasion of Afghanistan). These are the issues that steer the oil market, together with the price fluctuations resulting from individual and institutional speculations on commodities futures and options by the main financial markets (monetary crises).

b)   *"After the historical maximum of oil prices at the beginning of the '80s, the explorers applied new techniques of exploration and production; they have searched every inch of the world for new deposits. They have found few: the rate of discovery continued its uninterrupted decrease. There is only a finite quantity of crude oil and 90% of it has already been found" (here underlined).*
Sounds very dramatic, doesn´t it? Well, it's COMPLETELY FALSE.
On the contrary, after 1998, enormous oil fields have been found, both on- and offshore in the Mexican Gulf, Brazil, Angola, Sudan, India, Vietnam, Equatorial Guinea and Australia, amongst others.

c)   *"Exploration has been extended to the limit, and we have only to check the ocean trenches and the Polar Regions, where the possibilities are already known.*
This has already been refuted in the previous point, although it may be worthwhile adding that very recent discoveries of important oil fields are still awaiting data to evaluate their possible reserves. There are several areas in the world like the Great Lakes region of the African Rift Valley (Uganda, Tanzania and Kenya), the East African coastal platform, the Indian Ocean islands, or the Caribbean islands north of Trinidad (up to Cuba), where, until now, almost no geological investigation was ever undertaken. A chapter will be dedicated to these potential areas further on.

d)   *"We foresee the growth of the Caspian Sea production until the beginning of 2010 ... we coincide with other analysts ... that equate this zone's resources with those of the North Sea, that is, some 50 billion barrels, but never with the exorbitant amounts published in certain other media".*
Here the authors have "gone overboard" in a spectacular manner. The Caspian Sea production zones are reflected in the following data:

TABLE III - BRAZEN INCREASE OF OIL PRODUCTION IN THE
CASPIAN SEA (in thousands bbl/d)

A - South Caspian Sea (Baku Fields) production in years:

COUNTRY	1998	2007	2012
AZERBAIJAN	231	869	872
TURKMENISTAN	129	198	222
B - Northern Caspian Sea: Kazakhstan			
KAZAKHSTAN	537	1,484	1,728

Besides, in Kazakhstan, the two mega-fields of Kashagan and Tengiz have been evaluated, and in coming years, will increase the oil production of this country to well above 3 million bbl/d.

Regarding reserves figures, these two areas reach 56 billion barrels of oil reserves, and if we add the 6 billion barrels of the Azerbaijani Azeri-Chirag-Guneshli complex, and another 3 billion barrels of Turkmenistan, we reach a total of 65 billion barrels, much higher than Campbell and Laherrère's estimations.

Furthermore, the 65 billons bbl of reserves are "concealed" in well-known, well explored areas; but there are several other areas of oil potential in the Caspian Sea, and prospecting and discoveries are being carried on, so that this figure will probably fall short in the immediate future.

TABLE IV below, clearly depicts the gross mistake made by prophets of the doom, Campbell and Laherrère, based on King Hubbert's Peak Oil hypothesis. The table compares the real, 2012, aggregated oil production, with these authors' predictions, highlighting their error. The difference in world oil production is dramatic: 24.3 billions of bbl/year foreseen against 31.4 billion of real 2012 world oil production.

TABLE IV - THE ERRONEOUS PROPHECIES OF CAMPBELL AND LAHERRERE IN 1998 FOR 2012 (billion bbl/year)

THEIR FORCAST FOR	2012	Real production 2012
World production	24.3	31.4
Persian Gulf States	7.3	10.3
Ex-USSR	2.1	4.9

8 –JUST A FEW BELIEVE THERE IS STILL PLENTY OF OIL

The Australian Department of Infrastructure and Transport presented a report known as BITRE 117 published in 2009 but based on 2006 data. The interest of this report arises from its novel statistical method, which takes into account not only the classical evolution of the fields' oil production but also the historical evolution of discoveries. One of the most remarkable results in using this new technique is the fact that it achieves higher volumes of reserves than the officially recognized figures. Thus, for example, Russia attains 225 billion barrels, 3 times the official reserves of 77 billion bbl. A similar case is China, showing 80 billion bbl instead of the official 15 billion bbl. However, and in spite of this novelty, the report is not free of the peak oil "virus", claiming that the peak will be reached in 2016, although suggesting that the depletion curve will be smoother than the typical "Gaussian Bell" fall after the "peak". This report tumbles on the same basic missteps of the doomsayers: non-producing countries are ignored and no increased flow is gained by the use of EOR techniques.

Cambridge Energy Research Associates (CERA) is a consulting company that works for both private corporations and government agencies on issues dealing with energy and geopolitics. It was established by journalist Daniel Yergin, together with other experts on international politics. Its name is currently IHS-CERA, after the takeover by IHS, an enterprise centered on data processing and industrial know-how. Yergin and his agency are accused of positioning in favor of the interests of the large oil companies, and has always been considered a "super-optimist" by the preachers of doom. Yergin has denounced flawed prophesies many times and in his last reports he asserts that the world peak oil won't be reached before 2020.

A special "super-optimist" is Professor P. R. Odell, an economist who in 2004 published a book called: *Why carbon fuels will dominate the 21st. Century global economy*. His thesis maintains that there will be enough petroleum production to supply the growing world demand, basically because a great part of the oil consumption will be substituted by natural gas and not due to a general increase in petroleum production or yield.

On the other hand, the U.S. Geological Survey (USGS) completed in 2000 an exhaustive study that evaluates worldwide known and probable reserves as can be inferred from the geological parameters of well-identified sedimentary basins. This study reckons that there is sufficient oil to sustain the present rate of extraction for another 50 or 100 years, although it can't avoid the temptation of fixing a peak oil production for 2037. This prediction doesn't seem foolish, given the foreseeable rise in demand from many new economies, and in particular, the cases of China and India.
Campbell and other doomsayers think the USGS valuations are wrong (even thought, they have never won a single bet) and that the peak will be reached much sooner, (including the senseless claim that we are currently in a depletion scenario, crazy as it sounds).

It is worth remembering that the "experts" already alluded are probably the most relevant, both because of their professional authority and because their warnings and predictions stirred some impact on the public opinion. But there are many others who have taken sides with the fatalists and that weren't perceived with much interest by the media.

One of the last is Michael Moyer, who, in September 2010 published in *Scientific American* an apocalyptic article by the name of *How Much Is Left? The Limits of Earth's Resources*, where he states that the peak oil will be reached in 2014, with an extraction rate of 78 million bbl/day (2012 output was grossly 86 million bbl/day). (By the way. if you believe Mr. Moyer's predictions, you should be running to your broker to buy silver bullion or coins, because he also predicted that silver mines will be exhausted between 2030 and 2040).

Neither should we forget Yves Cochet, a French former Minister for the Environment, who, in 2005, in his book *Petrole Apocalypse*, predicted the conclusive decline of world oil output by 2010.

The following TABLE V abridges, with a speck of cruelty, the results of the "experts" catastrophic forecasts.

TABLE V - THE "EXPERTS" PREDICTIONS

Name or Organization	Year of Prediction	Peak Predicted in	Assertion as of 2012
King Hubbert	1971	2000	Wrong
Club of Rome (I)	1972	1992	Wrong
L.H. Ivanhoe	1995	2010	Wrong
Campbell-Laherrere	1998	2002	Wrong
M.S. Bakhtiari	2000	2007	Wrong
Club of Rome (II)	2004	2010	Wrong
D. Goodstein	2004	2010	Wrong
K.S. Deffeyes	2005	2005	Wrong
M. Simmons	2006	2009	Wrong
C. Skrebowski	2006	2001	Wrong
BITRE 117 (Australia)	2006	2018	Wrong
HIS-CERA	2008	2020?	Unlikely
Kuwait University	2010	2014	Wrong
AIE	2010	2006	Wrong
Hirsh Report	2010	2015	Wrong
EIA	2010	2016	Wrong
ASPO (last)	2011	2006	Wrong
D. Straham	2011	2006	Wrong
USGS	2000	2037	Likely?

It is worth recalling here, that many of the alarmists that usually call themselves "experts" are neither geologists nor economists, and most don't have a clue about oil exploration and never saw a derrick in their life.

This is the case of Charles S. Hall, a professor of environmental studies at the Syracuse University of New York, who, together with John W. Day, a professor of oceanography at the Louisiana University, published an article in *Scientific American* in October 2009 under the suggestive title of *The Limits of Growth, After the Peak of Oil.* The article, proliferates with all sorts of catastrophic forecasts like uncontrolled population growth and resource depletion, in consonance with the ideas of the "Club of Rome".

In their article they point out that the energy yield of oil exploration in the U.S. is becoming lower, as it has gone from 1 barrel needed to extract 100 bbl in the past, to 1 barrel to obtain 14 in 2000. They conclude that ... "in a few decades, this ratio will get closer to 1/1"... and it will no longer be profitable to extract oil. They forget that at least since 1950, the energy inputs have followed the same trend in every area of technological progress, from modernized, mechanical agriculture to mining. The amount of energy spent to obtain 1 bushel of wheat is, nowadays, some 20 times higher than it was in 1930, and, similarly, in those days, a 15 grams/ton gold mine was not profitable, while today, gold mines with only 1.5 g/ton grade are open for production.

JUDGE REAL WORLD OIL PRODUCTION FIGURES IN THE LAST 10 YEARS COMPARED TO THE CALAMITOUS FORCASTS OF TABLE V

YEAR	Million barrels per day	Billion barrels per year
2002	74.8	27.3
2003	77.6	28.3
2004	80.9	29.5
2005	82.1	30
2006	82.5	30.1
2007	82.3	30.1
2008	82.9	30.2
2009	81.3	29.7
2010	83.3	30.4
2011	84.2	30.7
2012	86.1	31.4

Estimated 2013 world oil production = 88 million bbl/d = 32 billion barrels/year.

PART B

WHAT THE RESERVES DISCLOSE

9 - WORLD RESERVES

By 2011, some 40,000 natural gas or oil fields were active worldwide, many of them being in operation for more than a century. Others, generally those with a low production (about 100 bbl/d or less) have alternated extraction periods with spells of idleness that usually coincides with bouts of low oil prices that made pumping uneconomic.

Curiously, 94% of world production comes from some 1,500 fields with gigantic reserves or mega-fields. Take into account that, for example, the Ghawar field in Saudi Arabia produces daily 6% of the world's total oil.

Accordance and disagreement on world reserves figures

The reserves figures presented in this book are the ones given in the BP Annual Report, and coincidental with the majority of international organizations and companies. Nevertheless, there are other published figures of countries or worlds' reserves that are much higher.

For example, the National Petroleum Council's (NPC) estimates that there are still 1,124 billion barrels of oil in place in the known sedimentary basins of U.S. territories, of which 374 billion bbl can be economically obtained using today's techniques. This amount represents about a quarter of the world reserves calculated for 2010, and 4.5 times the reserves formally calculated for the U.S. for that same year. If those numbers are correct, then the U.S. are in possession of the world's largest oil reserves.

But that is not all; recently, the U.S Energy Information Administration published a report on recoverable oil reserves in shale gas fields (Oil and Condensates in Associated Gas Shales) in continental U.S. (excluding Alaska) which indicated a total of 24 billion barrels (equivalent to 3.5 years' worth of U.S. oil consumption).

But what causes great disgust to, and blows the minds of doomsayers, is that the same U. S. Geological Service report underlines that the thick pile of sediments known as the "Monterey shales" contain THREE TRILLION BARRELS OF OIL ("in situ" oil). The Monterey shales underlie most of the costal band that extends between San Diego and Los Angeles, and are considered the "mother rock" that feeds most of the main Californian oil fields, (and considered responsible for the natural oil seeps that called the attention of the pilot Juan Rodriguez Cabrillo in 1542) (see ANNEX V). Today these shales are drilled basically to recover the natural gas and condensates associated to the oil in place, but new techniques are improving day by day to recover the oil in place.

If 10% of this oil volume were economically recoverable, it would mean that the American reserves would jump from the present, official 31 billion barrels to 331,000 billion barrels, a figure above the Venezuela or Saudi Arabia reserves. The problem is that, with today's available techniques, only between 1% and 3% of the oil contained in the Monterey shales is recoverable, although it should be pointed out that 1% is still 30 billion barrels, that is to say to double the current official reserves of the U.S.

TABLE VI, following, shows the world oil reserves according to BP:

TABLE VI
YEARLY OFFICIAL WORLD RESERVES (millions of barrels)

1980	667,000
1985	771,000
1990	1,003,000
1995	1,029,000
2000	1,105,000
2001	1,129,000
2002	1,190,000
2003	1,203,000
2004	1,209,000
2005	1,220,000
2006	1,234,000
2007	1,253,000
2008	1,334,000
2009	1,377,000
2010	1,383,000
2011	1,654,000
2012	1,669,000

2012 reserves of 1,669,000 million barrels is crude enough for 51 years at the current rate of consumption

TABLE VIIa - 10 COUNTRIES WITH THE BIGGEST RESERVES IN 1980 AND 2000 (in millions of barrels)

COUNTRY	Reserves 1980	COUNTRY	Reserves 2000
S. ARABIA	168,000	S. ARABIA	262,800
KUWAIT	68,000	IRAQ	112,500
IRAN	58,300	IRAN	99,500
MEXICO	47,200	EMIRATES	97,800
USA	36,500	KUWAIT	96,500
EMIRATES	30,400	VENEZUELA	76,800
IRAQ	30,000	RUSSIA	59,000
LIBYA	20,000	LIBYA	36,000
VENEZUELA	19,500	USA	30,400
CANADA	18,700	NIGERIA	29,000

TABLE VIIb – 10 COUNTRIES BIGGEST RESERVES IN 2012 (in millions of barrels)

COUNTRY	2012 Reserves	Years to supply the world at current rate of consumption
VENEZUELA	297,600*	10
S. ARABIA	265,900	9
IRAN	157,000	5
IRAQ	150,000	4.8
KUWAIT	101,500	3.4
EMIRATES	97,800	3.3
RUSSIA	87,200	3
LIBYA	48,000	1.5
NIGERIA	37,200	About one year
USA	34,900	About one year

At the end of 2011, the OPEC announced that Venezuela, with then reserves of 296 billion barrels, (enough to supply the world for 10 years at the present rate of consumption) had become the world's first ranking reserve, surpassing Saudi Arabia.

It should be noted that the first 10 countries represent 75% of the total world reserves, and the following 10 with outstanding reserves (over 10 billion barrels), about another 10%, with the remaining 15% being supplied by some 35 countries with really "low" resources (less than 7 billion barrels).

The latest estimations of the USGS World Assessment calculate the maximum world total reserves at 5,200 billion barrels (or 5.2 trillion bbl or 5,200,000 million bbl) tripling the figure of the "consented" volume indicated in TABLE VI.

10 – A USUAL LIE OF THE ALARMISTS: THE SHRINKING RESERVES

One interesting fact that can be found in the previous Tables is the following:
Over the last 30 years, the U.S. has managed to keep its reserves almost stable (36.5 billion bbl in 1980, to 35 billion bbl in 2012 in spite of being the worlds' third largest producer of oil, with an average of 8.9 million bbl/d, below Saudi Arabia's and Russia's 10 million bbl/d). This proves that when a country sustains it's exploration efforts, it is almost always possible to keep oil reserves more or less unaffected by the withdrawal (the U.S. pumps out about 3 billion bbl/year, roughly 10% of its' reserves). The U.S. example highlights the importance of the connection between volume of reserves and volume of extraction. As we have seen, if the U.S. were not discovering new fields daily, or improving the productivity of wells via Enhanced Oil Recovery techniques (EOR), it would run out of oil in 10 years.
One of the doomsayers' favorite arguments is that the ratio between reserves and production is decreasing on a worldwide scale. In other words, the speed at which new oil fields are being found to replace those depleted is slowing down. They love to show diagrams and curves that pretend to illustrate that no gigantic oil field has been discovered in the last 30 years, and that way, validate their argument that "world oil reserves are being constantly depleted since new fields cannot replace the oil withdrawal from the old wells".
However, this is completely false, since, as anyone can check in the yearly BP's statistics, from 1995 to the present, the ratio Production/Reserves has been stable, with values for the last 25 years, moving around an average of 40 years (years to consume the known oil reserves at current production rates). Besides, precisely in the year 2010, that ratio has reached a record of 43.5 years!

11 - THERE ARE SOME OIL WELLS THAT NEVER RUN DRY

The catastrophists always consider that when an oil field has attained a high production value and then starts to reduce production, it has entered an "exhaustion" or "depletion" phase, a situation that can't be reversed by any means and sooner or later (i.e. 2 or 3 decades) the field will be declared "dried out". However, there are wells or fields that have kept producing crude for many years after their "peak", some by simply pumping and others, with the most modern Enhanced Recovery techniques.
Just take a look to some astounding examples.
Although the Titusville well drilled in 1859 by "Colonel" E. Drake is considered the first oil well, there are documented precedents of previous operations using primitive drilling techniques.
The Chinese used hollow bamboo rods tipped with a "bit" or "burr" to dig into the ground and reach gas-bearing layers of sediments from were methane gas was drained out and burnt to boil and evaporate water from brines obtained from nearby salty springs; a clever move to obtain salts by saving firewood.
Since 1850, the association between salt and oil was evident in Pennsylvania, where wells were drilled to obtain brackish water from springs several dozen feet underground. Water actually poured from the well pipe "spoiled" with petroleum, by then deemed a bothersome muck.
The salt-petroleum association is so frequent that hydrocarbon deposits with no relationship with layers of salt or "evaporites" - a broader term that means layers of other salts like sulphates, chlorides, carbonates, etc., indicating a deposition of sediments in shallow and brackish waters in a hot and dry climate- are rare. Further on, we shall see the importance of "pre-salt" reserves, especially in offshore fields.
In 1848 (11 years before Drake) the Russian engineer F.N. Semyenov undertakes, with modest success, the first modern well drilling for oil on the Abseron Peninsula in the Baku region (Caspian Sea, today Azerbaijan).
Europe also predates "Colonel" Drake. In 1854 wells were being drilled for oil extraction in Poland, under the technical supervision of pharmacist Ignacy Lukasiewicz. Actually, there is some debate as to whether the first Polish wells were really "drilled", using primitive, cable-drawn "bits", as Drake did in Pennsylvania, or were typical mine wells dug by hand. Whatever the case, it is undisputed that in 1854, in the Carpathian region of Poland, close to the Ukrainian frontier, oil was extracted using modern methods. Until that year, the petroleum that seeped from natural springs was collected manually, a practice used since remote times, that is, digging shallow pits from which the mineral oil was removed with buckets or similar devices. Nowadays, the town of Bobrka, in the center of this Polish

region, has a small Petroleum Museum, where visitors can see an old well that still produces oil after 159 years.

Back to America: the first oil well drilled, if truth be told, was not the Titusville one (Oil Creek, Pennsylvania, U.S.A.), but one completed in 1858 (one year before "Colonel" Drake's), by J. Miller Williams in the town of Oil Springs, Lambton County, Ontario, Canada. This small town proudly exhibits a replica of the first American oil well. Also, several wells in the vicinity but not as old as the first one, are still producing oil, after more the one and a half centuries.

Even though the ecologists will have a tough time admitting it, oil extraction via drilled wells and pumping to the surface, has prevented two great environmental disasters. On one hand, oil wells were the salvation of sperm whales, a species that was close to extinction due to "overfishing". Sperm whales were much appreciated during the first half of 19th century for their "spermaceti", a grease or oil found in the bulge of the whale's head, that was used as a lighting fuel for lamps or for candle-making.

On the other hand, since the end of the 17th century, both in Europe and in America, many entrepreneurs started to open an increasing number of quarries and mines to obtain bituminous shales, that were later burnt and their gases distilled to obtain kerosene used as lighting oil: an expensive and environmentally dangerous practice. Had it not been for the drilling of wells to extract liquid petroleum, the quarries for bituminous shales would have had a strong impact on the European and American landscapes.

The first "petroleum crisis" occurred between 1878 and 1886, because kerosene lamps could not rival the electric lighting invented by T. Edison.

The crisis was solved straight away as new oil burners were adapted to boilers in ships and trains so that oil began to replace coal. In 1886, the invention of the automobile changed the world energy landscape, and since then, humankind started to increase its' dependence on "burning oil" or "mineral oil" spouting from the depths of the Earth.

As a child Pattillo Higgins frequently went to Spindletop hill (not far from the Texan coast) together with other kids, where they had fun sticking hollow rushes or canes into the ground close to sulfur-stinking, salt-water springs. They would then put a lighted match at the other end of the cane, and were amazed at the bluish yellow flame that would burn there for a while (we have already mentioned that the Chinese had been using this gas for centuries, also by means of hollow bamboo canes). Years later, as an adult, these children's games became an obsession. He was convinced that under the hill there was a rock that pushed on the layers of deep sediments where oil was stored. Incredibly, he was several years ahead of one of the most important geological discoveries about petroleum: the significant role of "salt domes", both in the genesis and in the accumulation of

The "Peak Oil" Myth Debunked

hydrocarbons.

At first, nobody would listen to him, until he became associated with Anthony Lucas, a naval engineer with some experience in mining salt rock deposits on the nearby Louisiana coast.

Finally, after several financial adventures while trying to obtain the crucial funds to drill a borehole, in January 1901, crude oil gushed from a 1,140 ft deep well.

Spindletop revolutionized an ancient industry - petroleum mining - that had been extracting mineral oil from wells barely 300 ft deep with maximum yields of 100 or 200 barrels per day. Till then, boreholes delivering more than a thousand barrels per day were thought extraordinary, with amazing cases of unusual wells in Baku yielding up to 3,000 bbl/d. In 1901, all the Baku wells spewed 212,000 bbl/d, a figure that in those days represented half of the world's production. But Spindletop's 1,140 ft well was gushing 5,000 barrels per hour! (120,000 bbl/d from one unique borehole). In those days, this singular well equaled the total amount of oil produced by all American wells. After the Spindletop discovery, the Texan wells helped to increase the world petroleum production from 500,000 bbl/d in 1900 to 1,250,000 bbl/d in 1915, and 4 million in 1930.

12 – SOME OTHER "OLD" PRODUCTION WELLS

In addition to the Oil Springs wells of Ontario, Canada, where a replica of the original derrick is protectively preserved, another long-lasting well is a well-looked-after one in Rouseville, Pennsylvania. It is known as the McClintock N° 1, and is located a mere ten miles from the famous Titusville well drilled down to 23 meters (75 ft) by "Colonel" Edwin Drake in 1859. McClintock N° 1 reached a depth of 680 ft in 1861 and, since then, has been in production for over 150 years. Although in those days it began producing 20 barrels per day, today it only gives 10 barrels per day in alternate months.

Even though it is not the longest-lived, the production at the Kern River field, which has been continuous since 1899, is the most famous case of historical oilfields that have been pumping oil for over a century.

More than 9,000 pumpjacks have been sucking oil out for more than a hundred years from this Californian field. It has been considered exhausted several times in the past, but its' present owner, Chevron, believes that after nearly 114 years producing a total of 2,000 million barrels, there are still 480 million barrels of recoverable reserves. An old forest of derricks, Kern River is an example of Enhanced Recovery using steam, which Chevron has been employing there for the last 50 years.

37

The first Kern River well started producing in 1899 and is still pumping today. After these many years, the field is still producing 75,000 barrels per day, occupying a very praiseworthy third position amongst the producing Californian oil fields. Its' volume of reserves will allow it to continue production, at today's rate, for at least another 15 years. Chevron's most recent figures estimate a total resource of 7,000 million barrels, from which only 30% has been withdrawn to date, so it would not be too risky to speculate on the possible recovery of 50% of the oil in place by using future and innovative Enhanced Oil Recovery techniques.

The first Kern River production "peak" was attained in 1904, when it reached a yield of 50,000 bbl/d. In 1980, secondary recovery was started using steam injection, reaching a second "peak" of some 120,000 bbl/d between 1981 and 2001. Then production declined to an average 79,500 bbl/d in 2010. Will there be a third "peak" before the definitive exhaustion in 2025?

FIGURE 2
KERN RIVER'S HISTORICAL PRODUCTION

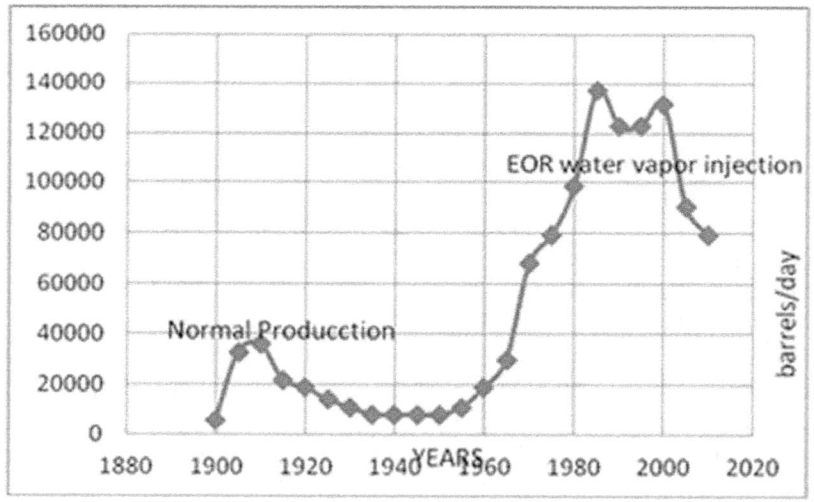

Enhanced Oil Recovery using steam at Kern River in an example of integral resource management. The injected steam is recovered as a mixture of oil and water at the well-head pumps. Once separated from the oil, the water is heated under high pressure and sent to an electric generator (gas-steam co-generation turbine), and the spent steam is pumped back into the recovery wells. Thus, the water is running in a closed circuit, and does not need to be replenished (apart from the losses in the process). Part of the recovered water is used for irrigation in the San Joaquin Valley. All of this is happening at only 95 miles from the megalopolis of Los Angeles.

Another "old stripper" can be found in today's Iran, the starter of the Persian Oil myth, the first oil well in that oil-prolific region. We are taking of Masjid Suleiman N°1 (the name translates as "Solomon's Mosque" although it was, more precisely, the ruins of a temple where Zoroaster's (a.k.a.: Zarathustra) followers adored the eternal flame) a discovery well that has been in production since 1908. M.S.N° 1, was the borehole that triggered the Persian oil stampede, since the enormous yield of this well and its successive neighbors defined the first oil field in the Mesopotamian region of Persia and the beginning of the "oil rush" into the Persian Gulf region. As soon as in 1911, - only three years after the oil discovery-, an oil pipeline to the port of Ibadan was already built, and shortly after the first refinery of the Near East was inaugurated there. Although the discovering company of the Persian Gulf oil was the Anglo-Persian Oil Company (a precursor of BP), the first technician to disclose the importance of the geological structures associated to well-known natural oil springs was the French geologist Jacques de Morgan, who, in a paper published in the *Annales de Mines* of 1892, pointed out the exceptional geological features in the region and called for action to start an immediate oil prospection.

Curiously enough, while the oil fields of today's Iraq and Iran went ahead at full steam at the northern end of the Persian Gulf, the geologists considered in those days that the coast of the Gulf (what today is Kuwait, Saudi Arabia, Qatar, Oman and the Arab Emirates), did not have any oil potential.

"I can drink all the oil produced in Kuwait" is a famous remark from a British Petroleum geologist back in 1936, after examining the logs of Bahara-1, the first wildcat drilled in Kuwait that proved to be a duster. Two years later, Burgan, the second largest oil field in the world was discovered.

The Digboi field is in the state of Assam, at the northeastern tip of India, not far from the Chinese border. In 1882, the Canadian engineer William L. Lake, assigned to the Assam Railways and Trading Company (AR&TC) noticed the presence of natural oil seeps, while overseeing the laying of the new railway tracks. He immediately tried to convince the company to begin prospect-drilling the area. Thus, the Assam Oil Company was formed, which managed to organize a team and drill the first oil well in India seven years later. It took one more year to get down to 663 ft where they hit petroleum. By 1901, Digboi had the first Indian oil refinery, and the city grew with typical European buildings, including an 18-hole golf course, which is still open. The oilfield reached its' peak production during WWII, with 7,000 bbl/d from its nearly 1,000 wells, both productive and dry. Since then, oil is still being pumped at the modest pace of 249 bbl/d, not too bad for a field that has been producing oil for over 120 years. Today the refinery is owned by the Indian Oil Corporation, and is considered the oldest in continuous operation of the world.

The USA strippers

The U.S. Department of Energy, the Pennsylvania State University and the University of Tulsa, together with thousands of "marginal wells" or "strippers" entrepreneurs are operating the National Stripper Well Association (NSWA) to help many small individual companies to achieve better extraction rates or to solve particular problems through collaboration.

Currently about one of every six barrels of crude comes from a "marginal" or "stripper" well, defined as an oil well that produces less than 10 bbl of oil per day. There are about 400.000 of those in the USA that together produce nearly 900.000 bbl/day.

Up to 70% of the oil retrieved from those reservoirs by the strippers may still be there. Waiting for new EOR techniques to be lifted. A future unknown reserve.

PART C

A PROMISING FUTURE

13 - IMPROVING RECOVERY AND DISCOVERING NEW FIELDS

The economist Leonardo Maugeri is deemed as the most famous director of the Italian oil company ENI (Ente Nazionale Idrocarburi). This expert is the exception amongst the pessimist doomsayers who predict the imminent end of the "oil era". In an article published in *Scientific American*, October 2009, with the suggestive title of: *Squeezing More Oil From the Ground*, he states that "there is plenty of oil for some time".
He coins such an exciting forecast primarily based on the fact that the world average recovery of the petroleum contained in the oil-bearing rocks of the earth's crust will reach 50% in the future, well above the current estimate of 35%. This high recovery of "oil in place" (by increasing the URR or ultimate recovery resource) will allow for a novel computation of the available reserves, from today's value of 1.67 trillion barrels to a future 2.17 trillion. At today's rate of consumption, this means 72 years more, or, taking into account the foreseeable growth in consumption, between 45 to 50 years more.
But L. Maugeri's somehow assumes that the peak will be reached much sooner, around 2030, by which time half of the world's available petroleum will have been used (for a recovery of 50%). From 2030 on, we will still have some 2 trillion barrels left for extraction, although from there, production rates will start to decline.
Another of L. Maugeri's key arguments is that we barely know a few of the thousands of oil-bearing sedimentary basins and their future reserves. In reality, the only thoroughly known basins at present are most of the plays in the U.S. (with the exception of offshore sequences), many of the European (except offshore Mediterranean and Atlantic) and a fraction of the Middle East basins (we will deal with this subject to a large extent further on).
Many of L. Maugeri's ideas and arguments were first presented in his 2006

book: *The Age of Oil*. Following his two fundamental criteria, we will now explain how the world will attain this PROMISING FUTURE of abundant fuel for several decades:

a) Production increase expected from Enhanced Oil Recovery techniques
b) Production from today's unknown, or mostly unexplored, sedimentary basins

14 - ENHANCED OIL RECOVERY TECHNIQUES (EOR)

This is the name given to assorted techniques devised to extend the life of a well or an oilfield. The title is usually abbreviated to EOR, and is often quoted as the acronym in many reports dealing with oil economics or hydrocarbon exploration. Generally, a distinction is made between "Secondary Recovery", that uses very simple techniques that have been continuously improving for over half a century and "Tertiary Recovery", that is one employing more sophisticated techniques and more expensive procedures to the point that it usually requires special conditions, and are, therefore, not suitable for every oilfield.
As is well known, conventional, vertical drilling techniques normally only allow for the withdrawal of between 20% and 35% of the oil "in place" or "in situ", -that is, the crude stored in the pores and micro-fractures of a "reservoir rock"-, the layer of sedimentary rock that contains the oil. The rare exception is the Kuwaiti Burgan megafield, where conventional techniques can recover up to 50% of the petroleum "in situ", held within an exceptionally porous and permeable rock.

The final amount that can be conventionally extracted by pumping depends on two fundamental factors:

a. The degree of permeability of the reservoir sediment (the number of interconnected pores that enable the movement of oil in the porous rock).
b. The viscosity (with respect to the density) of the crude oil. In the case of "heavy" crudes, natural recovery ratios are usually below 20%.

Trying to recover the oil remaining "in place" has spurred a lot of activity and research, an effort shared by every oil company in the world. Some of the original ideas became patents that were brought to the practical stage, and, once tested, became a wide variety of customary practices. These standardized procedures can easily adapt to different types of targets depending on the type of reservoir (i.e.: the sedimentary rock type, its porosity, the density of the crude, the pressure within the play, the oil/water ratio, etc.).

As always, the technique to be put into operation depends on its' economy or profitability. Obviously, priority will be given to those procedures that provide the highest yield at the lowest operational cost. This is a fundamental factor, because at times of high crude prices, such as nowadays, oil companies can risk the application of sophisticated and expensive techniques that will allow the extraction of a volume of oil which would not be profitable at lower prices.

According to published statistics, 95% of the 533,100 producing wells in the U.S. are using some sort of pumping system or EOR (Enhanced Oil Recovery) technique, with only about 27,000 being free-flowing wells.

Amongst the more frequently EOR techniques in use are:

Secondary Recovery Techniques   (Water or Gas Injection)

As petroleum is found as a layer of oil on top of a given volume of water, the forced injection of water or gas underneath the oil layer will put pressure on the latter, helping it to move upwards towards the extraction wells. This is very frequently done in fields where the gas obtained together with the oil withdrawal cannot meet a market end, and so it is re-injected into oil wells for secondary recovery (pressure build-up).

The most outstanding example of this type of secondary recovery is the megafield of Khurais, near Ghawar, Saudi Arabia. At Khurais, 22,600 million cubic feet per day (equivalent to 256 olympic swimming pools, or half the daily, domestic water consumption in Spain) of water (sea water) are injected to obtain an average of 1.2 million barrels of oil a day. In other words, a cost of about 4 barrels of water per barrel of oil recovered.

Khurais is an example of how a field can be "resuscitated", after having reached a "peak" of 144,000 bbl/d in 1981 with conventional pumping.

Khurais is the "bête noire" of the doomsayers, since it is a lively validation of HOW AN OILFIELD CAN INCREASE ITS' PRODUCTION AFTER HAVING PASSED ITS' CONVENTIONAL "PEAK".

While Khurais is an exceptional example that produces almost 10 times more oil after passing its "peak" and starting its "depletion", there are many other fields that have equaled, or are close to, their "peak" (maximum conventional yield) thanks to EOR methods.

Tertiary Recovery Techniques
1. Steam injection
In this case, the idea is to improve the fluidity of the reservoir's crude (i.e.

reduce its viscosity and make it more fluid) so that it can move more easily though the pores of the reservoir rock towards the extraction well.

The already mentioned Kern River field is a classic example of tertiary recovery via injection of steam.

2. CO_2 Injection

It is an alternative method that has the same goal as those described above, but with the advantage of using CO_2 as a gas propellant instead of steam, water or natural gas. CO_2 is a relatively cheap gas, easy to transport and use (liquefied or solid) and on top of it, its "burial" underneath is usually subsidized by governments committed to "CO_2 credits" (being a "dangerous greenhouse gas"). In brief, a great method that allows the tax-payers' money to flow easily into the pockets of the oil companies (both state-owned and private).

The Permian basin in Texas is famous for more than a billion of oil barrels recovered by CO_2 flooding.

3. Injection of nitrogen gas

An alternative to the previous, using nitrogen gas instead of CO_2. Often cheaper, being a by-product of the process to obtain oxygen, but more complicate to transport and handle than CO_2. Nitrogen is transported as a liquid and is gasified at the well's head. This technique is well known and is currently used for EOR of the Mexican Cantarell mega-field, currently producing 0.5 million bbl/d.

4. Chemical dissolution

As in the previous methods, a chemical compound (normally an acid) is injected through one, or several of the oilfield wells. The acid will react with the solid mineral grains of the reservoir rock and dissolve some of it, an event that will result in the increase of the rock porosity and permeability. In the case of calcareous (limestone) rocks, it has the added advantage that the chemical reaction produces CO_2 which, in turn, helps in lowering the oil's viscosity and increase the reservoir pressure. It is not a widely used technique for the reason that it's quite expensive, difficult to handle and causes the acid corrosion of the well pipes, valves and instruments.

5. Emulsifying chemical agents

It is the use of chemical compounds to reduce the oil's viscosity. It is not frequently used due to the high cost of the chemical products.

The U.S. Department of Energy has recently reported on the use of a surfactant polymer (ASP) in one of the wells at an oil field at Lawrence, Illinois, which has been in production since 1906. This EOR technique yielded an increase in production from the former 16 bbl/d to a present 70 bbl/d, and they have calculated that the same technique applied to the whole field would allow an increase in total recovery of 300 million bbl more, on top of the up to-date 410 million bbl yielded by the Lawrence field's. Although this is an early and unique test applied to a specific oilfield that improved production by 300%, one could guess that if this sort of EOR techniques are employed nationwide the U.S. oil production figures could jump to previously unseen numbers.

6. Bacteria

Although this technique is still in an experimental stage, it is deemed not only feasible, but also of a low environmental impact. It consists of incorporating into the reservoir a strain of innocuous bacteria that feed on the oil's more viscous fractions, metabolizing them into more liquid or gaseous products. In other words, the bacteria will fluidize the oil in the reservoir rock, making it easier to pump-up.

7. Pulse pumping (Power Wave)

It is a new, revolutionary technique, that involves water injection, but, instead of using a steady, continuous flow down the hole, the water is pressurized in a variable rhythm, or pulses, following a given frequency. This creates a vibratory movement in the reservoir rock's particles which, on one hand, lowers the oil's adherence to the rock, and, on the other, has an emulsifying effect on the oil-water mix, lowering its viscosity and increasing the flow towards the extraction wells. The most interesting thing about this method is its simplicity, as it does not need any element or accessory other than a special high-pressure pump which is moved from one well to the next. Obviously, the operating cost is very low and does not require a fixed installation. Even though this is a novel technique, it has already been tested successfully on some 175 wells in Canadian and U.S. oilfields, where it has increased extraction volumes up to 10%, which means a high profitability at today's expensive oil prices. The company that is exclusively operating this patented system is Canadian and called "Wave Front Technology Solutions"..

15 - NEW DRILLING TECHNIQUES (DIRECTIONAL, HORIZONTAL AND SLIM HOLE)

Although drilling techniques are not strictly EOR techniques, many of the new drilling methods can transform oil layers that were deemed unprofitable into feasible operations.

The new methods of directional drilling or horizontal drilling allow several hundred meters of the bore-hole contact with the reservoir rock formation, which, together with "hydrofracking" techniques, increase the porosity and permeability of the reservoir rock, i.e. actually "enhancing the recovery" from that well or field.

A specially interesting variant of this new technology is called SLIM HOLE DRILLING or COILED TUBING DRILLING (CTD). This is a high-speed drilling technique that drills wells of only 1.6 - 2.8 in. diameter, instead of the normal 3.5 - 5.9 in. and using a flexible pipe instead of rigid steel pipes. The main advantage being that the drill bit is not propelled by rotating the whole pipe from the surface (rotary table), since it has its own rotation motor and can be hoisted within its pipe whenever necessary to change a worn diamond bit. This saves a lot of time, the idle time lost in pulling up thousands of feet of steel pipes, unscrewing every segment, just to change the drill bit at the end and later lowering all the pipes of the drill-string back into the hole to restart drilling. Another advantage is that the smaller diameter of the well makes for quicker drilling. With today's equipment, it is possible to drill 330 ft per hour, which means finishing a 3,000 ft hole in only one day (24 hours shifts). An additional gain is that the borehole walls are always protected and the drilling mud can be pumped down even while changing the bit. The cost of a flexible pipe well is about half of the cost of a conventional (rotary) well. The method also benefits on the fact that the need of surface infrastructure is much reduced compared to conventional drilling, which makes this technique especially attractive for deep, offshore drilling, where the economics of size are crucial. Although the first tests were started some 25 years ago, the continuous advancement and improvement of CTD drilling is seen as a system that will completely replace conventional drilling in the near future.

The USGS estimates that in the Continental U.S. there are 407,000 million barrels confined in known sedimentary layers that cannot be extracted by conventional drilling. CTD drilling could recover at least 10% to 20% of that amount, representing more than one or two years of today's world oil production.

The Baker Hughes company has recently presented new techniques using conventional pipes up to 7.9 in. diameter, that allow for important changes in direction in one single operation, which also reduces drilling time. At one well, for example, the new system, patented under the name of "Carbo-Drill" allowed the completion of a 9,700 ft well in only 83 hours, which is a startling reduction in time and costs (a saving of half of the time for a deep, directional hole).

PART D

WORLD EXPLORATION IS STILL IN ITS INFANCY

16 - WHAT OIL EXPLORATION IS ALL ABOUT

To fully understand this chapter we must introduce some basic concepts on oil exploration.

The search for potential oil deposits implies a succession of steps which must be followed orderly until the final goal is clearly defined. The target is the location of a drill site where an exploration well will be spudded trying to reach the hosting rock or sedimentary layer that contains the oil, usually thousands of feet underground.

First stage: Geology or Surface Studies

1. The recognition of a big sedimentary basin (several thousand square miles in area), with at least 3,000 ft thick of layered sediments.

2. Geological survey of the basin, identifying the layers of "lode" or "mother rock", generators of oil (rocks rich in organic materials) and also the identification of the layers of "reservoir rocks" or "host rock", i.e. rocks with at least a minimum permeability and porosity and impregnated with hydrocarbons.

3. Geophysical studies (fundamentally seismic) to locate the structures that seem promising for the accumulation of oil in depth.

4. Modern auxiliary studies. There are several auxiliary techniques, both geophysical and geochemical, and multi-wavelength, satellite imagery analysis.

There is a remarkably interesting modern technique: detection of natural oil seepages at sea. Several companies specialize in the study of satellite or specific aerial photographs to target natural seeps both oceanic and in large lakes. As we'll see further on, natural oil seeps allowed for the discovery of the Cantarell submarine mega-field off the Yucatan Peninsula (Mexico).

Petroleum natural seeps and springs on land are normally well-known to the local inhabitants and there are many historically famous ones mentioned and depicted in different books and articles on oil history, from Marco Polo's description of the seeps at Asperon Peninsula (Baku) on the Caspian Sea's shore, to the location of the Titusville, Pennsylvania pioneer well by "Colonel" E. Drake in 1858 next to oil-oozing outcrops.

To detect those oil "slicks" that float on the water, indicating a possible connection to a seep on the ocean bed, several studies have to be completed which will sort out whether the oil is coming from a natural seep or from some accidental spill (i.e.: an old shipwreck). The shape of the stain, its' distribution, density, thickness, and drift course (impelled by both the shallow and deep marine currents) over several days or months will facilitate the pin-pointing of the natural seep on the ocean bed.

Amongst the most significant companies, we can mention "Astrium's Global Oil Seeps" which is a part of "Infoterra", a multinational company dedicated to worldwide geological and geophysical exploration. This company claims owning a database of 14.000 potential seepages slicks located around the globe.

Second stage: studies through well drilling

The drilling of exploration bore-holes is the last step of the geological exploration activities. A drill is the most necessary and decisive stage, the one that proves everything inferred or deemed from surface and geophysical studies, the last chapter that proves the presence or not of an economic crude pool at depth. This means the drilling of one to several wells, typically of some thousands of feet in depth using all types of instruments or sensors for monitoring all the variable physical and geochemical properties of the pierced layers. The object is to find out if the rocks bored into hold oil, its' physical and chemical properties, and what proportion of it can be pumped out. Samples of the cored sedimentary rocks can also be obtained for a more detailed assay in the lab. In some lucky strikes an exploration well can become a production well, like many historical "gushers".

Drilling a sedimentary basin is the fundamental and final step of oil exploration. It is IMPOSSIBLE TO ASSES the profitability of a field without the drilling data.

This means that there is no definitive evaluation of the hydrocarbon riches of a field, region or country until A LARGE NUMBER OF EXPLORATORY WELLS HAVE BEEN DRILLED in the most prospective areas. As a consequence no one can condemn extensive areas in the world as "oil barren" until a large number of exploratory wells are not spudded, even if not much hope is inferred from preliminary geological and geophysical studies. Dry holes are vital to scrap an area as "oil deprived". Libya was condemned for years as a barren country until venturous companies decided to take a chance. Sudan is a more recent and similar example.

In the case of world reserves, the worldwide number of exploratory oil wells is essential: we cannot figure out the reserves potential of the planet until most, - if not all - of the world's largest sedimentary basins have not been drilled to a minimum extent.

17. KING HUBBERT'S PARADOX

And here we come face to face with King Hubbert's paradox, as this geophysicist was relatively (and we insist on RELATIVELY) right in assessing the future reserves of U.S.A, and TOTALLY WRONG in trying to generalize his method to the rest of the world.

The fact is that, from 1859 to 1970, 80% of all the oil exploration wells drilled in the world were sunk within the U.S. territory. One has to consider that for more than a century, the U.S. was the major world oil producer (still in 1959, the U.S. was turning out about 50% of the world total).

In other words, in King Hubbert's days the U.S. was the only country in the world with plenty of statistically significant information and a high density of both exploration and producing wells that allowed for a statistically reliable forecast.

This is easy to understand, and quite obvious. Everyone knows that statistical reliability depends on sufficient data being evaluated. It is not the same trying to predict the result of an election from 1,000 interviews as from 10,000.

To make this perfectly clear, take the case of SENEGAL.

Senegal is an example of a poorly explored territory. This country has a surface area of 76,000 sq. mi., and, at the end of 2010, had only a total of 154 exploration wells drilled, of which 45 were offshore within its territorial waters (it has 325 mi. of coastline). This gives an average of 1 investigation drill per 700 sq. mi. of continental land. On top of it, the majority were shallow wells (normally less than 3,300 ft). All of which means Senegal must be considered "unexplored" today, even though it has a great oil potential, both inland and offshore.

An even more dramatic example is MALI. Although there were only a few and scattered geological studies over this vast country (479,000 sq. mi., located to the East of Mauritania and South of Algeria), they have put into evidence that the country has extensive sedimentary basins very similar to the rich hydrocarbon plays in Libya and Algeria. However, there have been only 5 oil exploration wells drilled, giving a density of just over one well per 100,000 sq. mi. This is equivalent to only 2 oil exploration wells drilled in Spain in the last hundred years. Unmistakably, Mali, should be considered, more than an unexplored country, as a "virgin" territory.

THE NUMBER OF WELLS DRILLED IN A COUNTRY IS A STRAIGHTFORWARD INDICATOR OF THE STRENGTH OF THE EFFORT INVESTED BY THAT COUNTRY IN OIL EXPLORATION, and is also a measure of the importance that the country's government has given to exploration (e.g.: there have been periods of several years in which Mexico has drilled less wells than Argentine, considering that Argentine is barely self-sufficient in oil, while Mexico is among the greatest petroleum producers and exporters).

All of this leads us to assume that there is an enormous quantitative difference between the exploration effort in the U.S. (and the consequent production and reserves, even if some people consider the country as "mature" or "declining") in comparison to the rest of the world.

NUMBER OF EXPLORATION WELLS DRILLED: THE KEY TO MEASURING A TERRITORY'S MATURITY AND, THEREFORE, ITS' POTENTIAL FUTURE RESERVES STILL LYING UNDERGROUND

To get an idea of the colossal difference in the available information that can be used in the prediction of future potentials, we can consider the historical data shown on the web page of the company Baker Hughes Inc.

18 - THE NUMBER OF ACTIVE DRILLS

This information comes under the title "Rigs Count", and it shows the number of active drills working (both landed and offshore), that are actually drilling the ground in each country (and, in the case of the U.S., each state) every month, although it does not include data from Russia or China. These numbers give us an idea of the exploratory effort underway in a given country or territory. It must be taken into account that there are periods of low activity, normally coinciding with historical periods in which the price per barrel is so low that the oil companies are compelled to reduce their expenditure on exploration. On analyzing this statistic we can notice that: Between 1975 and 2011, 50% to 65% of the total world bores were drilled within the U.S. territory. This enormous disparity can be seen clearly reflected in the two curves of FIGURE 3, which compares the number of rigs working in the U.S. and the rest of the world.

FIGURE 3: CONTRAST BETWEEN NUMBER OF RIGS DRILLING IN THE U.S. COMPARED TO THE REST OF THE WORLD

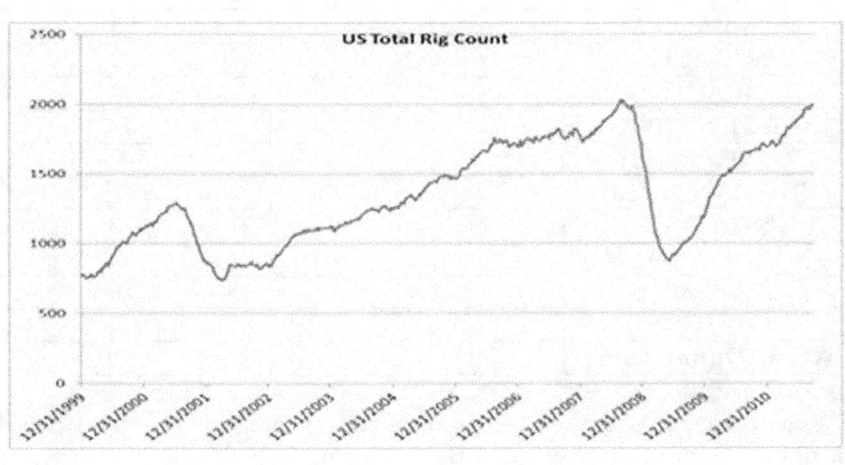

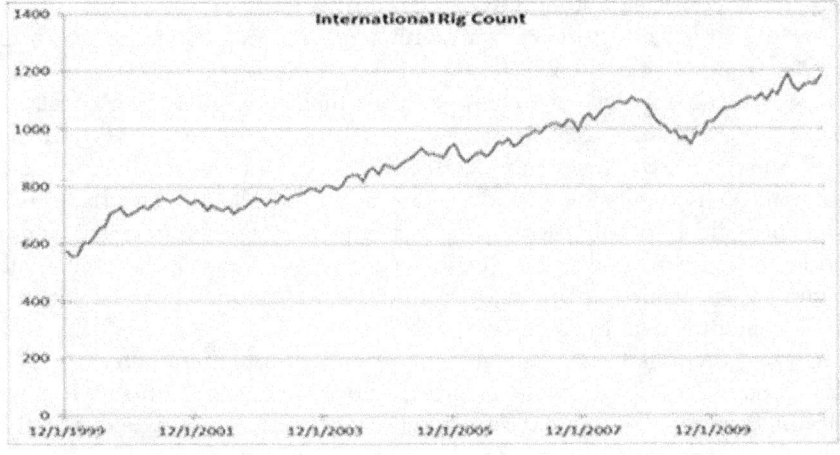

TABLE VIII shows that the number of rigs actively drilling in the U.S. in 2013 is visibly higher than in the rest of the countries, as, percentage-wise, the rigs active in the U.S. are 55% of the total active rigs in the world.

TABLE VIII - NUMBER OF RIGS ACTIVE January 2013(World Oil)

COUNTRY	ONSHORE RIGS	OFFSHORE RIGS
USA	1,756	53
CANADA	502	1
ASIA-PACIFIC	162	97
MEXICO	87	23
BRAZIL	30	43
ARGENTINA	69	0
VENEZUELA	64	6
PERSIAN GULF	295	37
NORWAY	0	22
POLAND	5	0
GERMANY	8	0
OTHERS	266	82
WORLD (non USA)	1,478	311

As can be seen, the data presented by World Oil Magazine for January 2013 is not different to the average of Baker Hughes stats for the last ten years, a fact that is consistently found over the last fifty years.

Note the Brazilian effort, with a number of offshore operating platforms not far from those in the U.S.A.

Norway is the opposite of Argentine: while the Norwegians aren't drilling a single hole on land, the Argentines are doing the opposite, and are not exploring their extensive continental shelf (although two British exploration companies have already found oil around the Falkland Islands – Islas Malvinas). It is worth mentioning that most of the Norwegian land is geologically unsuitable for oil deposits, with the exception of the shales around Oslo, while Argentine's territorial sea has boundless possibilities of harboring important hydrocarbon reserves.

Analyzing the Rigs Count data, it is interesting to note that Latin America is doing quite an oil exploration effort, with active rigs numbers not too distant from Canada's. Not surprisingly, Venezuela and Mexico, together with Brazil, are important producers and have substantial reserves.

U.S. and Canadian territory represent 15% of the total 52,397,152 sq. mi. of the continental surface area of the world (excluding the Antarctic continent), in other words: 7,572,622 sq. mi. Thus, it is easy to conclude that 60% of the oil prospecting effort is done on only 15% of the world's lands (and this was going on for 150 years), so that the rest of the planet can be considered HARDLY EXPLORED.

If we then subtract the number of wells drilled in the Persian Gulf region (Saudi Arabia, Kuwait, the Emirates, Iraq and Iran) the difference becomes even more outstanding. Broadly speaking, apart from the U.S., Canada, and the Persian Gulf states (especially the small ones), the density of oil exploration wells drilled IS SO INSIGNIFICANT THAT NO TRUSTWORTHY, DEFINITIVE ESTIMATE CAN BE DONE ON THE OIL POTENTIAL OF THE WORLD'S SEDIMENTARY BASINS.

Regarding the exploration in the Persian Gulf states, L. Maugeri makes a very interesting observation, signaling that between 1995 and 2004 there were 100 exploration wells drilled in this area while in the same period up to 15,700 exploration wells were spudded in the U.S. (besides the production wells). These differences are of prime importance when considering which countries or regions are sufficiently explored before stating the chances of finding new oil fields, as low or null. In many areas of the world the net, or grid, of wells is so widely spaced that no information can be gathered from extensive spans. It is in these zones where there is a high possibility of finding new reserves, especially when the surroundings have an oil "tradition" ("oil prone" in the industry jargon).

Another interesting fact: a total of 2,270,000 oil wells have been sunk in the U.S. over the last 100 years, while during the same span of time only some 8,000 holes were drilled in Saudi Arabia. If different land areas are taken into account, it can easily be inferred that in the U.S. there is one oil well for every 2 sq. mi., while Saudi Arabia has only one oil well for every 100 sq. mi.

To make this more outstanding, let's take a look at the estimated numbers of oil wells drilled in the world during 2012, according to the World Oil Magazine as shown in TABLE IX. As shown on the table, there are a total of 3,168 offshore wells, of which 8% will be off Brazilian shores and 7% in the Mexican Gulf (the rest will be in the North Sea, Angola, Gulf of Guinea, SE Asia, etc.).

The total number of landed wells drilled for the entire world in 2012, without U.S or Canada, is 45.744, and the total for U.S. + Canada is 58,628.

As we can see, it's "business as usual" with these two countries still representing 57% of the world's oil exploration effort (followed by China, with almost 23%). If we include the enormous land area of China, and discount the relatively fairly explored areas of the Persian Gulf states, we can safely say that 75% of the land surface of the world is unexplored, and if we include the oceanic basins, this percentage can reach 90 or 95%.

TABLE IX – WORLD'S NUMBER OF OIL & GAS WELLS DRILLED
DURING 2012

COUNTRY	N° Wells inland	N° Wells Offshore
USA	47,918*	355
CHINA	24,850	350
CANADA	10,710	11
Ex-URSS	7,827	84
Argentina	1,300	0
Mexico	1,195	59
Venezuela	705	10?
Brazil	610	253
S. Arabia	500	75
Australia	240	105
U. Kingdom	0	172
Norway	0	170
Colombia	120	0
WORLD (non US)	45,744	

* Between 1980 and 1985 some 80.000 wells a year were drilled in the USA,
representing in those days about 70% of the world total. The last USA record was in
2008 with 57,988 inland wells bored (mainly for shale gas)

CONCLUSION: WORLD OIL EXPLORATION IS STILL IN ITS
INFANCY

PART E

THE NEW OIL POWERS

Over the last 20 years several countries have made both a great exploration effort as well as innovations in Enhanced Oil Recovery within the scope of increasing their oil production. These are MATURE countries, that is, HISTORICAL PRODUCERS, who have been drawing up significant quantities of oil in the past (as rule of thumb, before 1990).

Another group of countries have revealed themselves as NEW PRODUCERS, that is, they weren't producing any, or insignificant quantities, of oil in 1990. We shall take a look at the first group:

TABLE XI compares the production increases between 1990 and 2012 of the 10 mayor "old" producers and the "new" ones.

19 - MATURE (HISTORICAL) PRODUCERS

CHINA

China has multiplied its' production by 1.5 times in the last 20 years, going from 2.77 million bbl/d in 1990 to 4.16 million bbl/d in 2012. Actually the Chinese effort is praiseworthy, because around 1960, it barely produced some 250,000 bbl/d and today it stands 5th in the top ten world oil producers.

It is quite possible that China will continue to increase its' production along with its' technical improvements in both exploration of new plays on land and offshore, as well as enhancing the secondary and tertiary recovery of oil from old fields. This country is compelled to increase its' oil production due to its' mounting dependency on imported energy sources demanded by the Chinese industry and economic survival. Over the last years the Chinese oil production has been growing at an annual rate of 7%, mainly resulting from both the exploration effort on land and in the vast Chinese Seas. Recently, the government has relaxed the stipulations for big foreign oil companies, tolerating a broader participation in all upstream issues of the oil business. This will permit considerable improvements for the declining yield of some of their oldest oil fields through modern Enhanced Oil Recovery techniques and especially by the use of directional and horizontal drilling.

Curiously enough, if by chance you browse through the pages of a very popular book written by the "expert" doomsayer, reporter Paul Roberts, titled *The End of Oil*, you can stumble into an hilarious sentence: "*... according to the analysts, China will never produce more than the 3.4 million bbl/d achieved in 2003.*"

QATAR

This small state (4,468 sq. mi., about twice the size of the State of Rhode Island), is an independent Emirate that doesn't belong to the federated United Arab Emirates. It is a flat and totally desert peninsula, some 100 miles in length, poking into the Persian Gulf. Like Kuwait, its' only resources are hydrocarbons, but, unlike the former, Qatar has never been an outstanding oil producer, with an average production of some 440,000 bbl/d in the years previous to 1990. The discovery of new oil-bearing structures has allowed a five-fold increase in production, which, in 2012, reached 1,968,000 bbl/d (a figure close to the current daily oil consumption in Germany = 2,358,000 bbl/d), combining crude oil and natural gas condensates. This spectacular increase in production ensues not only from the discovery of new, oil-bearing horizons, but fundamentally from Enhanced Oil Recovery techniques (EOR). This includes long, horizontal wells, very successfully applied at the Al-Shaheen field, which, thanks to this new technique, doubled its' production, from 240,000 bbl/d to 520,000 bbl/d in a few years. We should also mention that Qatar has gigantic natural gas reserves, sufficient to satisfy the entire European current consumption for 10 years. Qatar will probably increase its' oil production significantly in the future, although presently it is mostly dedicated to develop its enormous natural gas resources.

KAZAKHSTAN AND AZERBAIJAN

Both countries face opposite shores at the southern half of the Caspian Sea and both produce oil from the Caspian Depression, having spectacularly increased their productions over the last 20 years. Between 1990 and 2010 Azerbaijan has multiplied its' production x 4, from the 1990 254,000 bbl/d to the 1,037,000 bbl/d of 2010. Kazakhstan has had a threefold increase in the same period, from 551,000bbl/d in 1990 to 1,757,000 bbl/d in 2010.

Azerbaijan is multiplying the production by modernizing and re-drilling the ancient fields of Baku, where there are wells that still withdraw oil after operating for more than 150 years. While Kazakhstan has proven new fields at the northeastern tip of the Caspian, most of which have been discovered in the last 20 years.

ANGOLA

A recent African newcomer, this country, as well as Brazil, is one of the distinct examples of the outstanding results of modern exploration techniques, and of up-to-date production methods. Although the first exploration hole was drilled in 1915, when the country was under the Portuguese colonial rule, no oil was found in the coastal strip until 1955, when a meager production started. A few years later, the first shallow-water, offshore field was discovered in the Atlantic Ocean: Limba, in 1966. Even then, there wasn't much fuss until the first deep-water well was spudded 30 years later: Campo de Girasol, and finally, in 2002, the first ultra-deep-water field: Pluton. In 1992, when oil started to flow from the offshore wells, Angola passed the 500,000 bbl/d benchmark, but now, some 20 years later, its' production has multiplied x 4, and reached 1,883,000 bbl/d in 2010. It should be remembered that the expansion accelerated after 2002, when the country finally ended its longstanding civil war, almost never-ending, since their independence in 1975. However, although the main exploration effort is committed to the development of the known reserves located along the northern half of the Atlantic coast, some limited activity is starting in the southern offshore half, where some preliminary work indicate a fair chance of finding as much crude as in the northern half. On top of this, Angola also has several continental basins with oil potential still currently unexplored. We should keep in mind that the reserves calculated in 1990 for Angola's offshore were only 1.6 billion bbl, while currently the figure stands at 13.5 billion bbl, still far from the 88 billion bbl of total resources estimated by the USGS.

It is possible that in a near future Angola easily exceeds the 2 million bbl/d production mark, climbing to a high rank amongst the top world oil producers.

THE SPECIAL CASE OF RUSSIA

As we have seen, the Baku region (Imperial Russian territory in the 19th. century) was where the first oil wells were spudded, 11 years before Drake in Pennsylvania. Since then, and even in the Czar's days, Russia never stopped geological studies and mapping of its' vast territories and opening new oilfields, although at a much slower pace than other western countries. The forced industrialization after the 1917 revolution accelerated the exploration effort, but it was mainly centered on the westernmost region.

With an area of 6.6 million sq. mi., it has such a rich and complex geology, with as many potentially oil-bearing sedimentary basins as the U.S. and Canadian territories put together.

We should distinguish two regions. European Russia, to the West of the Ural Mountains, with a relatively high exploration well density, although lower than the U.S. or Canada, and with an important oil-tapping tradition, started over one and a half centuries ago in the famous Baku fields on the Caspian Sea (nowadays Azerbaijan) that are still producing a million bbl/d.

The other is the Siberian, or Asiatic region, extending from the Urals to the Pacific Ocean, a more recent oil development (broadly speaking, not earlier than 1950) with a much lower exploration drilling density that the latter.

Exploration activity was fairly reduced between 1990 and 2005, after the collapse of the industrial and administrative structure resulting at the end of the Soviet regime.

The statistics of the number of exploration wells in Russia are very unreliable and strongly biased according the quoted source, though in general terms, we can state that the Siberian region is still very far from a reliable density of exploration wells, something that translates as quite an unpredictable evaluation of its' resources.

In spite of this, the official oil reserves in Russia are still quite impressive: 77.4 billion barrels, far above the reserves figures of the U.S. and Canada added together (excluding the 143 billion barrels of the bituminous sands of Alberta, Canada).

The majority of the analysts agree that the Russian reserves are around 77 billion barrels, although there are higher estimates, like those presented by the former president of Lukoil, M. Khodorkovsky, or by the Texan consultants and analysts De Golver & Mac-Naughton, who stretch that amount to somewhere in the 150 to 200 billion barrels bracket, reserves that takes Russia to just below the top positions of Venezuela and Saudi Arabia.

As a consequence, we can expect many surprises in the coming Russian oil panorama, even without considering the enormous potential of the Arctic region.

20 – THE NEW PRODUCERS

These are countries that barely produced oil (less than 100,000 bbl/d) at the end of the 20th century but have now reached productions close to half a million bbl/d, after intense exploration efforts resulting in the discovery of new and productive fields.

BRAZIL should be in this group due to its' spectacular growth over the last years, but it will be considered apart (see ANNEX III).

THAILAND. This country has multiplied its' production x 5 over the last 20 years, going from 62,000 bbl/d in 1990 to 440,000 bbl/d in 2012. Nowadays, several multinational oil companies are investigating Thailand's offshore, amongst which is British firm Salamander Energy outstanding for their recent discoveries in the Bualuang Basin.

VIETNAM. The Vietnamese case is also praiseworthy, because it has multiplied its' production x 6 over the last 20 years, from 55,000 bbl/d in 1990 to 348,000 bbl/d in 2012. Vietnam has extensive territorial waters in the China Sea, where several productive oil fields have been located.

SUDAN did not produce ANY oil 20 years ago. It reached 465,000 bbl/d in 2010, basically from the southern region (Republic of South Sudan) which became independent from the Republic of Sudan in 2011. Geologically, South Sudan is very similar to the neighboring Libyan oil-rich basins; therefore, it is an area with great potential. The Melut Basin came into production in 1993 and has recently attained a rate of 486,000 bbl/d. The reserves of the known Sudanese fields are over 6.5 billion barrels, so it is highly probable that in a few years this country will be yielding over a million bbl/d. The Chinese petroleum company CNPC is very active there and is building an oil pipeline to the Kenyan coast on the Indian Ocean, thus freeing South Sudan from the costly, compulsory toll resulting from the use of Port Sudan as a shipping port for oil exports.

EGYPT is another example of a country making a hefty exploration effort. While the first oil well was drilled in 1910, it wasn't until some 50 years later that Egypt achieved a significant oil production of about 100,000 bbl/d. After reaching a "peak" yield of around 941,000 bbl/day in 1993, the fatalists considered the Egyptian fields on their way to "depletion". Since then it has slowly slipped its' production to the present 736,000 bbl/d. However, Egypt has never stopped increasing its' reserves, which today reach 4.3 billion barrels, enough to cover 16 years at today's rate of production. We must also consider the potential resources that could be uncovered under the deep "pre-salt" beds (Messinian) below the Nile River delta. There could be an estimated minimum of 5 billion barrels, which would allow an easy doubling of today's production, far surpassing the 1993 "peak". Recently, Apache Corp. announced impressive well results in the Western Desert where they are currently drilling with 25 rigs in their extensive concessions, with average yields of 2,000 bbl/day and several million cubic feet of natural gas.

THE CASE OF EQUATORIAL GUINEA

The Republic of Equatorial Guinea was born in 1968 from the former Spanish Territories of Guinea (Rio Muni and the islands of Fernando Poo). At the time, the oil resources of the region of the Niger delta (Nigeria) were thought to be important, but nobody could have foreseen that five years later this area would be producing over 3 million barrels of oil daily (almost doubling the current oil consumption of Spain). Of course, that these resources could extend to Bioko Island (Equatorial Guinea) was also unthinkable. In spite of this, a few years earlier some unsuccessful exploration work was done. Since the '70s, with the growing importance of the startling oil finds in the Niger delta and in the Cabinda region of Angola, Hispanoil (later, Repsol oil company) signed an agreement with the government of the new republic to form a novel company called GEPSA (Guineana Española de Petróleo) a joint venture company with 50% each for the Guinean state and Hispanoil. This company made surveys between 1975 and 1990, finding clear traces of oil in three of the four wells drilled, in the North offshore of Bioko Island, in waters only 200 ft deep. Due to political reasons and mainly because of the low oil prices in the 1985-1990 period, oil withdrawal was not considered commercial and the drillings were abandoned, including a gas field discovery named "Alba", that was later developed by Marathon Oil. Alba gas is today liquefied in a LNG plant in Bioko, producing nearly 0.2 Tcf a year. At the beginning of the 21st. century, some small American companies like United Meridian Corporation and Triton Energy drilled in the same region and announced the discovery of new fields, Today, the activity in Equatorial Guinea's territorial waters is intense, with the participation of large international oil companies like Chevron, Petronas (Malaysia), Mobil and Marathon. While the island of Bioko (770 sq. mi.) and the African territory of Rio Muni or Mbini (10,038 sq. mi.) make Equatorial Guinea one of the smallest African nations, the territorial waters between the two come to 23,200 sq. mi. An extensive area beneath which abundant hydrocarbon resources might be found. On the other hand, the sovereign territory of Equatorial Guinea includes the small island of Annobon which, although only 6.6 sq. mi. in area, is in the center of 92,665 sq. mi. of national waters, which could also be gifted with oil resources. This enormous extension of exclusive economic waters surrounds an island that is the geological and structural continuity of the oil shows located further North on the islands of São Tome and Principe (see PART F, following). This group of islands and the territorial waters surrounding them define a new area of high strategic value for hydrocarbon exploration in the Gulf of Guinea.

Today Equatorial Guinea produces 280,000 bbl/day with reserves estimated at 2 billion barrels (some 20 years at the current production rate).

PART F

THE "HOT" EXPLORATION ZONES

Some of the countries analyzed ahead, are not only in the preliminary stages of an intense exploration activity, but are also considered to be endowed by extensive and thick sedimentary basins with slight indications of oil or with striking similarities to other, neighboring areas where important reserves of hydrocarbons have been recently found.

Brazil is, again, one of the most archetypal countries in this sense. But, due to its' enormous oil potential, we will consider it in a separate chapter (see ANNEX III).

SUB-SAHARAN AFRICA

In general, and with the exception of the well-known oil fields of Nigeria, Angola, Algeria, Libya and Sudan, the rest of Africa is virtually an UNEXPLORED territory albeit with an extraordinary potential. As is the case with the rich fields of northern, or Saharan, Africa (Libya, Algeria, and to a lesser degree, Egypt), there are two zones in western Africa that have proved to be exceptionally fertile: Nigeria and Angola. Besides, as we'll see when dealing with the Gulf of Guinea, there are countless possibilities that these riches extend into the other Atlantic coastal countries. Although not strictly "Gulf of Guinea", there are four oil-producing countries whose geological features can be considered as a continuity of the already mentioned fields: Chad, Cameroon, Gabon and the Republic of the Congo (a.k.a.: Congo-Brazzaville).

But there are two more zones of great potential: one is defined at the southern coast of the Indian Ocean, and, in particular, the area encompassed between the continent and the island of Madagascar; the other is associated to the great tectonic depression - the Great Rift Valley - that is also gifted with thick and extensive sedimentary basins, some of which have already been proved to contain a promising oil potential, limited for now to Uganda, Kenya and Tanzania.

THE NORTHERN ZONE OF THE GULF OF GUINEA
It should not be confused with the "Niger River delta" of Nigeria. Actually, this extensive area of potential hydrocarbon resources has only been proven in a few spots, most of them still unproductive but where potential reserves have been indicated. The promising areas are defined along the Atlantic coast between SENEGAL and Nigeria, encompassing the following countries: BENIN, TOGO, GHANA, IVORY COAST, LIBERIA and SIERRA LEONE.
We must point out that in a first evaluation of the oil reserves made by the USGS (United States Geological Survey) in this area in the year 2000 (World Petroleum Assessment, 2000) the experts estimated one billion barrels yet to be discovered. But, in the following World Petroleum Assessment for the year 2006, this amount was multiplied by 10, indicating 10 billion barrels yet to be discovered. In spite of these impressive numbers, they are still far underneath the 132 billion barrels assigned to the Niger River delta or the 88 billion barrels estimated for Angola's offshore. Besides, one must take into account that the official reserves figures for the Niger River delta and Angola's are respectively 37 billion bbl, and 13,5 billion bbl.

Tullow Oil Company found oil in the Atlantic coastal strip of Ghana in waters some 3,300 ft deep, in the field called "Jubilee" in 2007. After developing the field, it was put into production in 2010, currently yielding 110,000 bbl/day. According to Tullow's estimates, and other international companies working in the area, the minimum, recoverable reserves in Ghana are estimated at 5 billion barrels. This makes mandatory a revision of the 2006 USGS's figures, considering that just one single oilfield shows half of the total resource estimated for a coastal strip that extends along 2,000 miles.
Nowadays, six fields have already been found in Ghana: Jubilee, Odum, Tweneboa, Teak, Mahogany and Enyenra.
Of course, the possible extension to the West of the reserves is also under exploration, in the territorial waters of Ivory Coast.
Several oil companies are also evaluating the oil potential of Liberia and Sierra Leone, both with geological features similar to the Ghana oil fields. Sierra Leone is being actively explored by several companies, such as Anadarko, Repsol, and Tullow, with two fields found to-date: Venus and Mercurio, both awaiting further development before being brought into production.

MORE SURPRISES IN THE GULF OF GUINEA: SÃO TOME AND PRINCIPE AND ANNOBON

The African Atlantic coast above considered is not the only "hot" area, with new surprises being announced every week, predicting its' transformation into an important production zone in the coming years. There is another promising zone in the Gulf of Guinea: the string of islands extending from the coast off Gabon to the island of Annobon. Curiously, these islands belong, surprisingly enough, to two different countries: at the northern tip, Bioko, the most important of the island territory of the Republic of Equatorial Guinea, about which we have already spoken.

Towards the South, and further out into the sea, two large islands are found: São Tome and Principe, today both form an independent country, after their liberation from former Portuguese dependence. Still further seawards, we come to the island of Annobon, barely 6.6 sq. mi. in area, and belonging to Equatorial Guinea. The natural oil springs of the São Tome and Principe Islands have been known for a long time. What's more, in the center of São Tome Island, where oil seeps from sandstone outcrops, a company called Island Oil made two drill holes in 1990. The deepest was the Ubabudo-1, cutting through 4,900 ft of sediments (mostly sands and clays interbedded with some layers of ancient volcanic flows). The majority of the sandy layers cut through by this well showed oil and gas traces, at the time not deemed sufficient to start a commercial attempt, although the hole never reached the bottom of the sedimentary basin. For the moment, no further prospection has been made of São Tome and Principe, although the territorial waters cover an area of 64,100 sq. mi., and natural slicks from the sea bottom have been detected on the water surface.

There is also an extensive strip limited to the Northwest by the island of Principe which will be explored, together with Nigeria ("Joint Development Zone"), because in this sector there is no agreement regarding the limits of the territorial waters between both countries. The demarcation of the JDZ began in 2004, and is thought to be the furthest extension of the oil-rich pools in the Niger River delta that made Nigeria attain the tenth position in the world ranking of oil reserves. Although there still aren't any productive holes in the JDZ, there are several companies interested in its' development. Chevron drilled the Obo-1 well in 5,700 ft of water where at least 150 ft of oil and gas net pay from multiple reservoirs were defined but still pending on future developments. Chevron estimates a total of 14 billion barrels of oil reserves in the JDZ and several companies are planning to deep-drill the area.

If we look at a map of Equatorial Guinea, we shall see, some 190 mi. to the Southwest of Bioko Island, the island of Principe; a further 90 mi. South from this, São Tome and finally some 60 mi. seaward the small island of Annobon. These four islands: Bioko, Principe, São Tome and Annobon are of volcanic origin, like the Canary Islands, and others of the Atlantic Ocean, such as Madeira and Cabo Verde.

But, wait a minute: didn't we study in our high-school text books that it was impossible to find oil accumulations in volcanic regions? How can islands formed by successive layers of lava and volcanic ejecta, contain "reservoirs" of oil if, a few centuries ago, they were still spewing forth incandescent lavas?

There is still no absolute answer to this paradox, but it seems that the islands emerge over the sea surface because they "crown" large structures which "core" is made essentially by sediments. As if they were the snowy peaks of large mountains, what can be seen on the surface is only the volcanic "peak" (the snowy, white summit), while underneath, there is a great mass of sedimentary rocks (the big, grey mountain beneath the snow-covered peak). And it is precisely in this great sedimentary structure where we find the most favorable conditions for the accumulation of hydrocarbons.

NAMIBIA AND SOUTH AFRICA

The so-called "Orange Basin" which extends the marine platform North and South of the limit between South Africa and Namibia has many geological similarities to the oil-prone structures found on the slope of the Atlantic platform facing the stretch between Santos (Sao Paulo) and Rio de Janeiro, in Brazil. A number of offshore wells sunk years ago in a zone situated 105 miles from the Namibian coast, and which led to the discovery of the Kudu gas field, have proven an important, and as yet not fully appraised, sedimentary basin that holds oil systems. Today, seismic studies are being undertaken in the region in the scope of defining promising oil-bearing structures.

SOUTHERN INDIAN OCEAN REGION

Several countries in this region seem to be oil-endowed and awaiting for a great future.

MOZAMBIQUE. In mid-2011, the Italian oil company ENI discovered a large conventional gas deposit in the northern offshore of Mozambique, in the so-called Rovuma Basin. The first estimates indicated an enormous potential of 15 Tcf. Although initially it is considered as a natural gas play, there are traces of oil in many of the prospection wells, and the chances are that sooner or later an oil field will be found. This seems to be pretty realistic, considering that Mozambique extends for 308,900 sq. mi., as well as the favorable odds resulting from its' vast sedimentary basin lying at the depths of its territorial waters of the Indian Ocean, still barely explored.

The Rovuma Basin is also under scrutiny by the American company Anadarko, which has already completed several deep wells in the Lagosta and Camarao fields, all with abundant conventional natural gas (reserves estimated at 30 Tcf) together to some oil shows.

Mozambique has a coastline of more than 1,240 miles that defines a broad strip of territorial waters with some 193,000 sq. mi. in extension that is still virtually virgin to oil exploration, except for the northern end (Rovuma Basin) and a reduced fraction of the southern tip (Mozambique Basin).

Keep in mind that, as well as the discovery of the great gas fields, several submarine oil seeps have been detected in the same region, indicating deeply-lying hydrocarbon systems.

MADAGASCAR. Although the natural oil springs were well known to the local tribesmen since old times, it wasn't until the dawn of the 20th century when modern exploration started. Soon, expectations vanished when only very heavy oil was found, so thick that no reliable market was found suitable for such a remote wealth. This gloomy picture is nowadays changing thanks to the efforts sustained by a private Malagasy company: Madagascar Oil. Up to the present 69 wells have been sunken in the Tsimiroro field, where an extraction pilot plant, using steam injection is in operation. This company, now associated to Total, the French multinational conglomerate, has also located traces of lighter oil plays, easier to draw up if commercial volumes are appraised.

However, much greater potential awaits offshore, over vast territorial waters in the Indian Ocean that should be auctioned off to big oil companies as soon as the island achieves a minimum political stability.

SEYCHELLES, FAR MORE THAN JUST LAVISH TOURS

The Seychelles are a cluster of some hundred islands which are actually emerging granite mounds that have resisted marine erosion and that stick out over the rest of an extensive, submerged, sedimentary basin. It is part of a continental slice that detached from the African plate when the African and Indian plates moved apart while opening the Indian Ocean. This slab of continental crust stores several sedimentary basins that extend over a total surface of 502,000 square miles! (2.5 times the land area of Spain).

On such a vast area only 4 exploration wells have been sunken in the last 50 years, and, - hard to believe - all of them went through thousands of feet of sediments with traces of oil and gas. Nowadays, several geophysical campaigns are underway trying to pinpoint the most attractive geological structures that would deem some exploration drilling. Keep in mind that Madagascar, less than 650 miles to the South of the Seychelles has 30,000 million barrels of tar sands reserves (of a lower quality than the Canadian or Venezuelan oil sands) and that natural tar balls are continuously being washed up onto the paradisiac beaches of the area.

UGANDA

Several companies are exploring the region. Tullow Oil and Heritage Oil are drilling in the Lake Albert zone, where a number of oil-prone layers have been found. Some, like the Kingfisher well with an exceptional yield of 13,000 bbl/d, are prematurely producing. The potentially rich Ugandan region is located in the tectonic depression of the Great Rift Valley, a large geological structure which will probably become a rich oil play in the coming decade.

KENYA

Previously discovered riches in neighboring countries like Uganda to the West and Sudan to the North warrant similar possibilities to Kenya and are spurring exploration. The geological frame of the Kenyan basins shows an auspicious potential for the formation and storing of petroleum. In that scope and since 1950, several wells have been drilled in the Turkana Lake basin and the Lamu Embayment, only detecting, -for now-, uneconomic oil shows, since no viable accumulations have been defined to the present. Kenya also has a great offshore potential in the Indian Ocean, where several holes have been spudded, with a number of successful outcomes like the Lamu Basin where according to Pancontinental, an Australian oil and gas prospecting company, a total of 3.7 billion barrels of oil and 10 Tcf of natural gas are estimated from geophysical appraisals. Recently, the Chinese CNOOC company has joined the search of other western exploration companies.

TANZANIA

Tanzania is an example of the inadequate assessment effort committed to sub-Saharan countries. Only 40 oil exploration wells have been drilled, and although rich natural gas deposits have been found, no commercial oil plays have been defined as yet. The most interesting area, where prospection is focused, is in the northern extension of the gas-rich Mozambique Rovuma Basin within Tanzanian territorial waters. As is the case with Mozambique, besides the discoveries of large gas deposits, the Tanzanian waters of the Indian Ocean have frequent shows of submarine oil seeps and slicks, an indication of offshore hydrocarbon deposits at depth. Also, like other East African countries such as Kenya, Uganda or Mozambique, there are abundant and promising opportunities in Tanzanian Rift Valley locations in inland areas.

THE CASE OF THE AUSTRALIAN CONTINENT

AUSTRALIA is a nation-continent that, world-wide, ranks sixth in land area, first as a coal exporter and third as a natural gas exporter. Unfortunately the country is not so well endowed in oil deposits, although the current production is not too bad at 568,000 bbl/d, yet quite far from their year 2000 "peak" of 809,000 bbl/d. But, as we'll see, this was possibly a transient "peak", considering the auspicious expectations of new discoveries.

The first oil exploration well was dug in 1866, but after a few unlucky, isolated attempts, no organized and technically proved geological exploration campaign was started until after the WW2. Wapet was the name of the oil company organized by Australian entrepreneurs associated to the Californian Standard Oil Company that started the first geophysical appraisals in a selected number of sedimentary basins. The first production well on the continent was spudded in 1953, immediately followed by the discovery of new, commercially viable fields, and especially after 1963, with the development of the first offshore field.

The Australian sedimentary basins are enormous; the Carnarvon Basin, for example, covers 44,400 sq. mi. on land and another 206,500 sq. mi. (the land surface of Spain) under the Indian Ocean and down to a depth of 11,500 ft. However, until now, it's been the smaller basins, such as Cooper or Eromanga than have proven more fertile.

Anyhow, Australia can be deemed as a poorly explored territory, considering that the total number of oil exploration wells drilled since 1946 (the previous ones were just anecdotic) come to barely over 2,000, unevenly distributed over the 2,934,400 sq. mi. of continental land mass to which a further equivalent area of territorial waters has to be added. This sadly compares to the average of 60,000 exploratory wells drilled in the U.S. in the same period and over a surface that is only 20% larger than the Australian continent and resulting in an average of one exploration well per 58 sq. mi. in the U.S. against one per 1,467 sq. mi. in Australia.

Pondering these figures there is no doubt that, oil-exploration-wise, the Australian continent is still in its' infancy.

NEW ZEALAND This island country is in a way a similar but more dramatic example than Australia and, oil-wise, can be considered an unexplored country.

Although formed by two main, large islands, all exploration efforts since 1934 were limited to the southwestern tip of North Island, where the Taranaki Basin is located. There, 499 wells have been drilled, and today produce some 55,000 bbl/d of oil and gas. To the contrary, only some 50 unsuccessful exploration wells have been drilled in the Eastern Basin, on the other side of the island, where, in spite of the evidence of carefully pinpointed 300 natural oil and gas springs, no commercially viable accumulations have ever been found.

Many ignore that the extensive New Zealand archipelago, with a total extension of some 104,250 sq. mi. sticks out over a large marine platform of

579,200 sq. mi. (three times the land area of Spain) where more than 30 sedimentary basins have been identified. The potential of possible offshore fields in its' territorial waters has barely been evaluated and could hold great surprises.

SOUTH AMERICA
BRAZIL. Together with Africa, this country is today one of the "hottest" regions for oil exploration. Although limited to a short stretch along the extensive Atlantic Brazilian coast, the estimated offshore reserves for the short interval of 300 miles of coast between Rio de Janeiro and Santos (Sao Paulo) is about 50 billion barrels of oil. However, the geological framework of this segment is very probably repeated over the thousands of miles of Atlantic coastline between Uruguay in the South and the Guineas in the North. In fact, several oil basins along this coastal strip are already in a productive stage, like: Espiritu Santo (North of Rio de Janeiro), Reconcavo and Bahía Sur (South of S. Salvador de Bahía), Sergipe-Alagoas offshore (South of Recife), Ceará and Potiguar (region of Fortaleza) and Margen Continental (in the Amazon delta).
Brazil oil endowment is analyzed in more detail further on, in Annex III.

GUINEAS – a.k.a. GUYANAS
The "Year 2000 World Petroleum Assessment" authored by the USGS (U.S. Geological Survey), indicates a potential 15 billion barrels for the Atlantic marine coastal strip that faces the three Guyanas.
In 2011, Tullow Oil, the discoverer of the Jubilee field in Ghana in 2007, and its' associate, Shell, announced the discovery of an offshore oil horizon, some 93 miles seawards, in waters 6,500 ft deep in the Atlantic Ocean. This being, for now, the only oil discovery in French Guyana waters to be commercially evaluated, until future exploration wells prove the estimated figures of the USGS.

JAMAICA AND THE ANTILLES, A VIRGIN POWER
Both the continental platform and the continental slope to the South of the island of Jamaica have been recently pointed out as important sedimentary basins with great hydrocarbon potential. In this case and as for now, there is basically very scarce geological information with the exception of several natural oil seeps detected in the region. Curiously enough on the Jamaican coast (Saint Anne's Great River) there is a famous, burning methane "chimera" that is worshiped as a mythological beast by the local "rastafaris". (More on "chimeras" in ANNEX II).
The same can be said about the coastal platform over which stand the Barbados Islands, to the North of Trinidad and Tobago, currently the objective of intense geophysical prospections.

PERU is a clear example of immature exploration. Up till today 18 sedimentary basins with high hydrocarbons potential have been identified in this country, but only a third of those are undergoing significant exploration activities and only 3 are currently producing. In 2011 only 19 exploratory wells were spudded, and yet that same year Peru imported 15 million barrels of oil.

FORECASTS ABOUT THE ARCTIC
In 2008, the USGS completed an evaluation of the potential of the conventional oil and gas deposits North of the Arctic Circle. Using cutting-edge statistical methods and a plethora of information about the geological settings of 33 selected sedimentary basins in this region, they tote up 90 billion barrels of oil reserves, plus another 44 billion barrels of gas condensates, i.e. a total of 134 billion barrels of liquid hydrocarbons, a figure that equals almost 10% of the world reserves calculated for the year 2010. They also estimated that 84% of this amount would be taken from offshore fields. Later, a group of experts updated the Arctic evaluations in the USGS-2012 Report, showing new figures that result in Arctic oil reserves amounting to 300 billion barrels or 22% of the world's oil yet to be discovered. Furthermore, they have also assessed countless reserves of natural gas: 1,669 Tcf, which represent 1,391 years of the present Spanish consumption, or 15 years of the world's gas consumption, for 2010.

OLD EUROPE
Although it would seem that no surprises can be expected from a continent whose geology is known in minute detail and where limitless exploration wells have been drilled through the years (albeit at a much lower density than in the U.S.), Statoil, the Norwegian state company surprised the media as well as the most highly professional circles with its' latest discovery in the North Sea.
To the chagrin of the fatalists, by the end of 2011, Statoil announced the discovery of the new Johan Sverdrup field in a North Sea area where no-one thought that a new oil field could be found. This wasn't the result of sheer luck but the outcome of a long-planned exploration effort. The Norwegian oil company never ceased in its' pursuit to find new, productive structures in the Norwegian Sea and at the western end of the Barents Sea. And it's doing quite well, since it has located several structures that will soon be carried to production. Two new fields have been discovered in the Barents Sea that total 500 million barrels, and geological evidence of much more.
As for the new Sverdrup field in the North Sea, the preliminary estimates indicate an average of 1,500 million recoverable barrels, which represent

20% of the present Norwegian reserves, with a possible increase of those figures in the very near future. Actually, the Norwegian exploration effort is praiseworthy; during 2011, 54 offshore wells were drilled, which led to the discovery of 22 new fields, with a total of 3,300 million barrels of new oil reserves. The majority of those finds were in the North Sea, although three are located in the new and promising Barents Sea region.

Other companies are prospecting at the western margin of the North Sea (West of the Faroe Islands, and to the West of Ireland).

Anyway, there are still several virgin, offshore areas in Europe, like most of the French and British Atlantic coasts, which could hold some surprises. The same can be said about the Black Sea and the Mediterranean.

In fact, several gas-holding mega-structures have been recently discovered in eastern Mediterranean, like the 25 Tcf found in territorial waters of Israel, and similar reserves to the South of the Island of Cyprus. This could validate the existence of an oil system in the easternmost quarter of the Mediterranean Sea, in accordance with the numerous, natural upwellings of natural oil found at several points at sea in front of the coasts of Syria and Lebanon. Some experts consider that the presence of large volumes of gas stored in the sands of the Upper Tertiary in this region, also known as the Levantine Basin, could indicate important accumulations of oil in deeper, Mesozoic sediments below.

PART G

PEAK OIL (PRODUCTION) OR PEAK OIL DEMAND?

Surprisingly, and against the Peak Oil Production that, today, the doomsayers are postponing for 2017 or 2025, many of the most developed countries in the world are today confronted with a new reality: the Peak Oil Demand.

A surprising fact crops up when analyzing the world oil consumption statistics: most of developed, industrialized countries are diminishing their oil consumption.

Different experts call this modern trend: the Peak Oil Demand.

TABLE X below shows the main industrialized countries that have seen a noticeable reduction in oil consumption in the last decades.

Some industrialized countries like Canada preserved a flat demand over more than a decade due to the growing importance of natural gas, hydroelectric and nuclear power plants that replaced oil-burning electrical utilities.

In the U.S.A. a sharp reduction of fuel consumption in electrical utilites was one of the driving forces, with an electrical generation demand in 1975 of 1,7 million bbl/day falling to a mere 200.000 bbl/day in 2008, mainly replaced by coal-fired and, more recently, natural gas co-generation.

Japan is a similar case, choosing nuclear power generation to replace oil-burning utilities, a situation that has been knackered after the 2011 Fukushima disaster.

Oil demand is extremely variable as a function of economic development and per capita Domestic Product. The U.S. burns 23 barrels of oil per head per year, while India only uses 1 bbl/head/year and China 2.5. European countries and Japan consume about half of the U.S. needs: between 10 and 14 bbl/head/year. On the other hand, semi-industrialized countries like Brazil, Colombia or Argentina are placed in-between: about 5 bbl/head/year.

TABLE X – PEAK DEMAND BY COUNTRY (million bbl/day)

COUNTRY	Year of Peak Demand/Need	Needs in 2012
OECD countries	2005 = 50.1	45.6
Europe & Eurasia	1990 = 23.2	18.9
USA	2005 = 20.8	18.6
European Union	2006 = 15.1	12.8
Japan	1996 = 5.7	4.7
Russia	1989 = 5.1	3.2
Canada	2007 = 2.3	2.4

It is interesting to compare two highly industrialized countries: Canada consumes 23 bbl/head/year while, with a similar climate, Finland only needs 15 bbl/head/year. Russia, also highly developed, burns only 7.5 bbl/head/year, somewhere between little industrialized countries and the European average. The relatively low figures in oil consumption by the Russian Federation are probably related with its high hydroelectric and nuclear power plants as well as an important number of coal-burning utilities.

Cars and, in general, road transportation, are a heavy load on petroleum consumption and considered by many experts a major factor to explain oil consumption differences between European countries (Russia included) and the US or Canada: North American "gas guzzlers".

AVERAGE GAS CONSUMPTION PER VEHICULE

COUNTRY	Liters / 100 km	Miles per US gallon
USA	10	23.5
China	7.6	32
India	5.7	39
France	5.5	44

Most of the U.S.A. SUVs (sport utility vehicle) makes less than 15 mpg (i.e. over 20 liters/100km). Opposite to this, many new conventional or hybrid car models are performing in the 40 to 50 mpg bracket, about matching the European fuel efficiency.

This tendency towards a boost in fuel efficiency in personal cars is adding to the increased trend of using natural gas as a fuel in heavy vehicles and electrical utilities and explains the continuous drop in oil consumption since 2005. It must be considered that every millions of barrels of oil saved in the U.S.A. allows for an equivalent increase in non-industrialized countries like China or India. In fact OECD countries are, on average, diminishing oil consumption at a rate of 1% per year while non-OECD countries (mainly China, India, Indonesia, Brazil, Pakistan, Nigeria, Bangladesh and Russia, making 50% of the world population) are increasing about 3% per year. This means that an average of 2% a year in oil consumption can be expected in the next decade, that is, roughly 2 million barrels more per day.

Recently, Seth Kleinman, the head of energy strategy at Citigroup remarked that engine technological advances are improving fuel efficiency at a 2.5% annual rate worldwide (about 3.5% in automobiles and 1.5% in trucks), enough to constrain the oil demand.
On top of this, low natural gas prices in the United States are pushing both transport companies and individuals towards natural gas burning cars and trucks, relieving market pressure on oil products.

"Peaked" or not, many countries are substantially increasing their oil production. As in previous chapters it is worth distinguishing between "old" producers: countries that produced more than 1 million barrels/day for the last 22 years; and "new" producers: those that almost DUPLICATED their oil production in the last 22 years.

TABLE XI - CONTRASTING PRODUCTION INCREASE BETWEEN OLD (HISTORICAL) AND NEW PRODUCERS (million bbl/d)
OLD PRODUCERS

COUNTRY	PRODUCTION 1990	PRODUCTION 2012
Russian Federation	10.4	10.7
Saudi Arabia	7.1	9.5
USA	8.9	9.2
China	2.8	4.2
Iran*	3.3	3
Iraq**	2.1	2.9
Mexico	2.9	2.9
United A. Emirates	2.3	2.6
Venezuela	2.2	2.5
Nigeria	1.9	2.1

* Recent Iran oil production was severely jeopardized by the UN sanctions
** Iraq is very slowly recovering a normal production due to social and political unrest

NEW PRODUCERS

COUNTRY	PRODUCTION 1990	PRODUCTION 2012
Brazil	0.6	2.2
Angola	0.5	1.8
Colombia	0.4	0.9
Oman*	0.7	0.9
Sudan	0	0.5
Ecuador	0.3	0.5
Vietnam	0	0.4
Equatorial Guinea	0	0.3
Yemen	0.1	0.3
Congo Republic	0.1	0.3

* Oman was producing about 0.3 bbl/day in the 80's

ANNEX I

SOME MEGA-OILFIELDS

Although the majority of the world's oil wells produce less that 20,000 bbl/d, there are a small number of fields with exceptional productivity, over 100,000 bbl/d, and an outstanding group of fields that supply over one million barrels per day: the Mega-fields or Super-structures. We have already seen the GHAWAR phenomenon in Saudi Arabia, the largest of all the world's oil fields, but a few others are not too far behind.

Let's take a look at some of them.

BURGAN

Kuwait's most important oilfield, discovered in 1938, but not exploited until 1946, is considered the second largest oil field in the world, behind Ghawar (Saudi Arabia). Its' total recoverable reserves are evaluated as 90 billion barrels, of which 26 have already been pumped up, leaving at least a further 20 billion recoverable (Burgan has privileged recovery ratio of almost 50%). It is presently producing 1.7 million bbl/d and the EIA calculates that its' yield in 2020 will drop 4% to 1.64 million bbl/d, although it is foreseeable that, from 2015 on, EOR (Enhanced Oil Recovery) techniques will be put into operation to preserve the present flow. It should be pointed out that the issues concerning the total reserves of this mega-field are constantly being contended by the doomsayers, although most of the Middle East Oil experts agree on the above-given figures. A few of them also emphasize that the future completion of EOR technics may result in unexpected surprises in both yield and reserves.

KHURAIS

This is a mega-field close to Ghawar in Saudi Arabia. Discovered in 1957, it wasn't put into production until the '70s. It reached its' "peak" (so to speak) in 1981, with 144,000 bbl/d, and for years, its yield was kept up to an average of 68,000 bbl/d. A few years ago, the SaudiAramco oil company undertook a complete study of this field, and decided to make an enormous investment to bring it to the present production of 1,200,000 bbl/d. To achieve this yield, an average volume of 4.5 million barrels of seawater is injected (i.e.: some 25 million cubic feet) daily. (see more details in PART C, point 14).

IRAQ. As is the case of Saudi Arabia, this country holds a great number of very high-producing fields, although somewhat lessened by the fortunes of wars and economic conflicts. Nowadays, important multinational companies are deploying up-to-date techniques to improve yields in the RUMAILA, MAJNOON and WEST QURNA and other gigantic fields, and bring their present productions to a total of 8 million bbl/d. This is foreseen to be completed by 2020 and, thus, Iraq will move to the third position in the world producer's ranking, easily doubling China or Iran figures. On the other hand, it must be stressed that Iraq is far from being a thoroughly prospected country, but is rather a poorly explored one. It couldn't be any other way when one considers that between 1980 and 2010 Iraq has drilled only ten exploration wells! During 2012 only about 2,000 wells were spudded in Iraq of which only some hundred were real wildcats. As a consequence, many experts claim that only 25% of its potential reserves have been found or evaluated.

RUMAILA is considered to be the 4th mega-field in the world, and is now producing over one million bbl/d, half of Iraq's production. At the moment, the field is being developed by a consortium formed by BP and the Chinese CNPC to treble its' production in a few years.

MAJNOON is an exception in the Iraqi oil history, being a field discovered in 1975 by a Brazilian oil company. Although its' present production is low, a consortium of important oil companies hopes to reach 1 million barrels daily in a few years.

Regarding WEST QURNA, even though today it barely produces 500,000 bbl/d, large multinational companies like Shell and Exxon are improving the production capacity to bring it up to 2 million bbl/d.

BAGHDAD EAST is another supergiant holding 9 billion bbls of oil according to official measured reserves. However it is producing only 10.000 bblpd, while development is compromised due to the fact that most of the deposit is located underneath the residential areas of Baghdad City.

KIRKUK is currently producing about 700,000 barrels a day of oil while its reserves are estimated around 17 billion bbl. It is one of the oldest fields discovered and producing in Iraq.

ZUBAIR is another supergiant in the Basra region, although holding more than 6 billion bbl of oil reserves it's currently producing only 200,000 bblpd. The Italian oil company Eni, the main field operator at present, estimates to reach a 1.1 million bbl per day plateau within four years.

According to Dr. Hussain Rabia's report published in World Oil in 2007, some 64 giant and supergiant oil and gas fields were discovered when serious exploration seismic and drilling started during the '70s. By 2007 only 23 of these 64 were actually developed and put on production. In his report the HALFAYA field is considered one of the most attractive supergiant fields awaiting for development, with reserves of 16 billion bbl of oil and 9 Tcf of natural gas, this field could easily sustain 250.000 bopd.

The author concludes that potential Iraqi oil reserves may be as much as 324 billion barrels, more than double the official reserves figure (see TABLE VIIb) and far above Venezuelan reserves.

KASHAGAN

This mega-field is located in the northern end of the Caspian Sea, in the Republic of Kazakhstan, in waters that barely average 33 ft deep. Discovered in 2000, it has total (provisional) reserves estimated at 30 billion barrels (equivalent to one year of the world oil consumption), of which only 9 billion (30%) are thought to be recoverable. It was brought into production in 2012, and its' objective is to reach a 1.5 million bbl/d average by 2020.

TENGIZ

Land-locked, but very close to the shores of the Caspian, and neighboring the new-born Kashagan field, Tengiz was discovered in 1979, and began production in 1993. With total reserves of 25 billion barrels, some 6 billion (25%) are considered recoverable. It is today producing at a rate of 450,000 bbl/d, but Chevron wants to increase the withdrawal to 540,000 bbl/d by the end of 2013. Some doomsayer state that this field had reached its' "peak production" in 2010, but this is utterly false. The limiting yield of this field is tied to the fact that the crude has a high sulfur content that cannot be commercialized, and has to be stocked above ground waiting future use.

MARACAIBO LAKE (VENEZUELA)

Under the northeastern end of this enormous lake (brackish, as it is connected, at it's northern tip, to the Caribbean Sea) lie the fabulous Maracaibo fields, discovered by Shell in 1914 and brought into production in 1917. Almost a century of production has left behind a forest of derricks, dumb witnesses to the 7,000 extraction wells that pump up hydrocarbons from this field. Its' recoverable reserves have been estimated at some 30 billion barrels, so that a very long life awaits this oilfield producing an average of 2.5 million bbl/d.

TUPI (LULA) - JUPITER

Located in the Atlantic Ocean some 170 miles off the coast of Rio de Janeiro, Tupi was discovered by Petrobras in 2006, closely followed by Jupiter, in January, 2008. A joint commercial operation from these two fields began in 2010, with an initial output of almost 100,000 barrels per day, which will be increased to 500,000 bbl/day before 2020. The exploitation of these reserves, estimated at 30 billion recoverable barrels, is done from floating platforms, over a water depth of 6,500 ft, at the bottom of which the production piping cuts through another 16,400 ft of rocky formations before hitting the oil-bearing strata.

CARIOCA-PAN DE AZUCAR is another offshore mega-field facing Sao Paulo, Brazil, which is thought to hold 40 billion barrels of oil.

SAMOTLOR is the most productive Russian field which reached a peak of 7 million barrels per day in 1980, currently down to only 750,000bbl/d (more than the whole production of all the Argentinian oilfields). Several companies are planning to increase its' yield to almost one million barrels/day.

In Iran, the FERDOWS-MOUND-ZAGHEH field, was discovered in 2003, and presumably holds 10 billion barrels of recoverable reserves. For known and obvious reasons, its' exploitation has not started yet, but plans are drawn to obtain a future yield close to a million barrels daily.

AZADEGAN is considered the largest oil filed in Iran with 33 billion barrels of oil in place but currently producing only 40.000 bbl/day.

ANNEX II

CANTARELL, OIL, METEORITES AND POCKMARKS

Cantarell is an offshore mega-field that kept Mexico amongst the main world oil exporters for two decades. It is located in shallow waters in the Mexican end of the Gulf of Mexico, (some 190 miles to the west of the port of Campeche, in Yucatán). Discovered in 1976 by PEMEX (the Mexican state oil company that has a tight monopoly both in the exploration and the production of hydrocarbons in Mexico), it began production in 1981 and reached its' "peak" in 2004 at 2.14 million barrels per day (almost half of Ghawar, and almost as much as Burgan). Its recoverable reserves are calculated at 18 billion barrels and, thanks to EOR techniques, it is today producing half a million barrels daily.

<u>Natural oil seeps: common ecological disasters?</u>
This field presents two very peculiar features: it was really discovered by the fisherman Rudesindo Cantarell, who was complaining that in his fishing grounds in that zone of the Gulf of Mexico, the submarine oil seeps were scaring off the fish. His complaints reached the ears of Pemex's geologists, who checked that, true enough, there were important emissions of hydrocarbons from under the sea bed.

It is interesting to note that the natural submarine oil seeps are quite frequent everywhere in oceanic waters, and their identification through special aerial photography or satellite images is an important tool for the location of offshore oil deposits. Many of the submarine sources of oil frequently have an associated ecosystem of animals, algae and other micro-organisms with a peculiar metabolism, using hydrocarbon compounds liberated into the sea in their own benefit. Most ecologists consider oil spills into the sea, both those caused by shipping accidents and those originated by oil drilling or exploration platforms, as "catastrophic events". Although these accidents are regrettable, and usually have a higher media impact than an environmental one, we should not forget that natural seeps are quite frequent all over the world's oceans, being an event that has happened for eons in the geological history of our planet. Inland oil seeps or bitumen springs have a local impact that is less severe than submarine oil upwellings, that need a fairly long time until a new biological equilibrium is established in the spill zone.

A study undertaken by NASA has revealed that in the U.S. part of the Mexican Gulf, there are around 600 submarine springs which spew forth some four million barrels of oil per year, half of which reaches the surface while the other half is metabolized by submarine bacteria and other microorganisms.

Coal Oil Point, located along the northern margin of the Santa Barbara Channel (California) is considered one of the world's largest and best studied, natural hydrocarbons seeps in the world. Investigations carried out by the Earth Sciences division of the University of California estimate a release of 2.000.000 cubic feet of natural gas (mostly methane) a day plus some 100 daily barrels of oil. (More on Coal Oil Point oil seeps at the end of Annex V).

<u>The Chicxulub meteorite and others.</u>

The other odd fact about Cantarell oilfield is that its' reservoir rock is a very porous rock formed by a gigantic explosion: the Chicxulub Impact Crater. In fact, 65 million years ago, a great meteorite impacted in this region of the Yucatan peninsula, producing a global catastrophe which caused the extinction of numerous animals and plants, amongst which were the famous dinosaurs. On impact in this zone, the meteorite formed a crater of several miles in diameter, which was quickly filled by the rocky debris, and which, millions of years later, holds a great volume of hydrocarbons: the Cantarell oil field.

But Cantarell in not he only example of a hydrocarbon deposit stocked in the debris left by the impact of a meteorite. There are several other known examples, like:

1. The Arbuckle deposit, in Ames, Oklahoma, U.S.A. This oilfield is currently producing, with a total of 11 million barrels of oil and a steady flow of natural gas already withdrawn. Curiously enough, the impact breccia that holds the hydrocarbons is made of granitic fragments.

2. The gas and oil field of Calvin-28, near Calvin township, Cass County, Michigan, U.S.A., with 600 million barrels of oil reserves emplaced with a brecciated impact structure of 4.5 miles diameter.

3. The Des Lacs hydrocarbon deposit, also known as the "Newporte Field" in North Dakota, U.S.A.

4. The Barrow gas field, on Alaska's northern coast, also called the "Avak

structure".

5. The Marquez gas field in Texas.

6. The Elsinore gas field, a.k.a. the "Sierra Madera" structure in Pecos, Texas

7. The gas deposit at Lyles Ranch in Texas.

8. The oil deposit at Red Wing Creek, North Dakota, U.S.A which has produced, up to present, some 13 million barrels of oil and significant amounts of gas. Reserves are estimated at 70 million barrels.

9. The oil and gas field at Steen River in Alberta, Canada, that produces 600 bbl/d.

10. The oil and gas field at Viewfield, in Saskatchewan, Canada, with a production of 400 bbl/d.

11. The Boltysh Crater in the Ukraine.

The Boltysh Crater is located about 150 miles southeast of Kiev. It has 15 miles in diameter and at the moment of the impact the meteorite unearthed a depression of about 2,000 ft depth, later filled with Tertiary (Paleogene, some 60 million years BP) continental sediments. Wells drilled through these deposits proved the existence of at least 1,200 ft meters of organic rich lacustrine shales that contain several layers of oil shales and shale oil. Curiously the age of this impact is only a few thousand years younger than the Chicxulub.

12. Shiva is a submerged impact crater located in the Mumbay Offshore Basin of the Indian Ocean, measuring some 300 kilometes in diameter and filled with 4 miles of marine sediments rich in organic matter. It contains hydrocarbon reserves estimated at 8.5 million bbl of oil plus 24 Tcf of natural gas.

13. Although there is no total agreement among the experts, most of them believe that the Bedout Structure located near the northern coast of Western Australia (actually the name comes from the Bedout Island, nothe of Port Hedland). Bedout is a submarine crater 160 miles in diameter with its typical internal structure confirmed by seismic and some of the oil wildcats that were drilled through the impact breccia. Moreover its 250 million years age coincides with the Permian-Triassic boundary and associated extinction event.

POCKMARKS

Meteoritic Crater depressions are different to very similar but smaller structures found in ocean floors and usually called "pockmarks". This depressions are made by gases, normally methane, that ooze from marine sediments at the sea-floor while changing the flat or nearly flat bottoms creating small dips, usually about 60 ft in diameter and 10 ft of maximum height. Sporadically they can be larger, like the one found in La Have Clay in the Scotian Shelf (part of the Continental Shelf located Southwest of

Nova Scotia, Canada) measuring 900 ft long, 400 ft wide and up to 50 ft in depth. The biggest pockmark described was found at the bottom of the Belfast Bay in the Gulf of Maine, measuring near to 1,000 ft in diameter and 100 ft maximum relief within an extensive cluster of pockmarks (about 60 pockmarks per square mile).

Pockmarks were first described on the continental shelf offshore Nova Scotia (Canada) by King and MacLean in 1970 and since then described in most of the sea-floors all over the planet. The majority of earth scientists relate these pockmarks with gas escapes or gas seepages that can be associated or not with oil seepages, since many of the occurrences have been related to biogenic methane rather than oil-related natural gas (thermogenic gas). Of course, not all the gas or oil seepages at the bottoms of the oceans form pockmarks. The number or spatial density of pockmarks can be highly variable: form 500 to 100 per square mile. In some cases the rims or the inside of pockmarks are filled with algal mats, bacterial aggregates or even deep sea corals.

In many cases pockmarks are indicative of an oil or natural gas play underneath and merit further exploration efforts such as deep 3D seismic and/or geochemical prospection of the seeping gases and eventual oil seeps in the vicinity.

ANNEX III

SOUTH AMERICA: BRAZIL, ARGENTINA, URUGUAY AND COLOMBIA

THE CASE OF BRAZIL

Brazil started its' search for oil quite late, in 1930 (when Argentina was already producing oil from several fields), and minor yield of 200,000 bbl/day was obtained by 1980. From then on, the first developments of the continental basins in the Northeast (Sergipe-Alagoas) enabled to raise production to 600,000 bbl/d. It was then that the first offshore prospections started, in front of Rio de Janeiro (Campos Basin) in Atlantic waters, at first in shallow waters, and soon daring into waters over 3,300 ft deep. The offshore finds made in the strip approximately between Rio de Janeiro and Santos (Sao Paulo) allowed production to grow to over one million bbl/d in 1995 and to over 2 million bbl/d in 2009.

According to the US Energy Information Administration (EIA) Brazil will be producing 6.4 million bbl/d in 2035, and will probably be 6th. on the world ranking (today, together with Norway, it occupies 13th. position).

Remember that the enormous reserves (estimated between 50,000 and 100.000 million barrels) are located in the offshore, Atlantic zone, extending over some 300 miles approximately between the cities of Rio de Janeiro and Sao Paulo. But these deposits are not exclusive to this zone, and, in fact, may be repeated in any other sector along the thousands of miles of the Brazilian Atlantic coast. The present limits, evaluated by hundreds of deep drill-holes, and from which, nowadays, over one million bbl/d are extracted, is only ONE TENTH of the potential extension of the coastal strip. Not only are there no geological reasons to exclude a future "Tupi" or "Carioca" in front of Fortaleza, Bahía or Porto Alegre, but, to the contrary, the geological history of the sedimentary basins on the continental epi-margin rather suggest a probable high degree of success in those areas. The geotectonic conditions for the generation of hydrocarbons, and the possible existence of sedimentary layers bearing profitable quantities of oil are equivalent, and it is very possible that, in a near future, Brazil will once again surprise the world with new, Atlantic mega-field discoveries.

Together with the discovery of important volumes of new reserves, another prominent fact that oil exploration along the Brazilian coast disclosed is the presence of oil-rich layers underneath a thick (over 7,200 ft) layer of massive salt. This opens up enormous future possibilities, not only for both shores of the Atlantic Ocean, both South American and African, but also for similar finds in the Mexican Gulf, where the first deep wells, deep enough to get under the thick salt layer, are been drilled.

The Amazon Basin is, for the most part, a sedimentary basin with potential hydrocarbon resources. The westernmost portion of this vast extension holds the so-called "Solimoes Basin", from which Petrobras is now withdrawing some 45,000 bbl/d of oil and gas in the Juruá-Urucú region. Take into account that, in spite of this, Solimoes is unexplored, as, to the present, only 78 exploration wells have been drilled over a total surface area of over 193,000 sq. mi. (the land surface of Spain), resulting in a density of exploration wells of one every 2,471 sq. mi., which means that Solimoes can be considered practically "virgin".

The region known as Juruá-Urucú-Chibata has reserves calculated at 1,000 million barrels. The Juruá well, drilled by Petrobrás in 1978, discovered substantial natural gas reserves, enough to justify the laying of a gas pipeline which supplies the city of Manaos (population 1.6 million). Curiously enough, the Amazon oil deposits are also "sealed" by a thick layer of salt, like the "Pre-salt" mega-fields offshore of Rio de Janeiro and Sao Paulo.

THE ARGENTINIAN CASE

Argentina reached its' production "peak" in 1998, at almost 900,000 bbl/d. From that year on, production declined to the present 600,000 bbl/d. Keep in mind that, during a century of oil exploration and production, a "mega-field" has never been found in Argentina. All of its' oil fields are of a low yield, with wells that rarely produce over 1,000 bbl/d. The majority of the fields are between 100 and 50 years old, and, at most of them, secondary and tertiary recovery techniques are used.

On the other hand, and to the contrary of Brazil, the exploration of the extensive Atlantic continental platform (one of the most extensive in the world), encompassing several thousands of square miles, and an average depth less than 660 feet, has never been systematically explored. Only isolated, low-resolution, geophysical campaigns have been undertaken. Insofar as well drilling is concerned, only about 20 wells were spudded between 1980 and 1994, but none reaching more than 3,300 ft deep. Even so, some of the wells, like the Calamar X-1, drilled by Exxon 155 miles

West of Tierra del Fuego, had an initial yield of 3,200 bbl/d), and showed several intervals with traces of oil or gas, that were not followed or further evaluated in any detail.

This compared to the British and international companies that drilled the so-called Malvinas (Falkland) North and Malvinas (Falkland) South Basins, they made 22 drill-holes, down to over 9,800 ft, with preliminary estimations of reserves in the order of 1,500 million barrels The majority of the wells found stretches with traces of hydrocarbons, and one of them attained a flow of 5,508 bbl/d in the initial pumping tests. In both Malvinas areas, intense geophysical campaigns were undertaken, using special high-resolution seismology, leaving no doubt that great expectations must be awaited in this vast territory of about 400,000 sq. mi.

On the other hand, the most recent drilling, on the Vaca Muerta – Los Molles Formations, in Neuquén, an attempt to evaluate the potential of the "shale gas", in view of the continuous decline of the natural gas reserves in Argentina, has evidenced a new, "non-conventional" oil resource that accompanies the gas. According to the latest EIA evaluation of the Neuquen Basin, recoverable reserves of the crude contained in the "oil shales" are estimated in 27 billion barrels, which represents more than ten times the Argentinian "conventional" oil reserves calculated for 2012. The production of the future field could reach 100,000 bbl/d, which would increase the present national production by 15%. Other more optimistic calculations indicate oil reserves of 50 billion barrels; in other words, multiplying by 20 the current conventional oil reserves.

VIRGIN URUGUAY

In the neighboring República Oriental de Uruguay, the offshore potential has been deemed more seriously, and several geophysical campaigns have been made related to the exploration drill-holes "Lobo" and "Gaviotin" done by Exxon in the '70s in territorial waters less than 650 ft deep, in the so-called "Punta del Este" Basin. Curiously enough, although both holes were deemed dry and abandoned, they had various traces of oil and gas, especially those located in formations from the Carboniferous to the Cretaceous periods, similar to those that hold hydrocarbon-bearing sequences in the Brazilian Santos and Campos Basins.

Uruguay never produced oil or natural gas.

COLOMBIA

The third South American producer after Venezuela and Brazil, Colombia is a clear example of the absurdity of Oil Peak theories. Oil production started quite late compared to its neighbor Venezuela, where the famous Maracaibo Lake deposits were found in 1914, with the first wells drilled in

1942. Production steady climbed to a "peak" of 838,000 bbl/day in 1999, followed by a decline to around 600 thousand bbl/day until 2008, when more liberal policies were adopted by the government allowing for multinational exploration rights. Production escalated to 950,000 bbl/day in 2013 and is projected to attain more than 1.5 million bbl/day in 2020 as new leads are developed both inland and offshore. Colombian proven oil reserves are not very substantial, calculated in 2,200 million barrels, but is a book example of poor investigation: between 2004 and 2011 only an average of 30 exploration wells per year were drilled, a situation that quickly changed to the current 130 prospecting drill-holes/year spudded since 2012.

Cusiana-Cupiagua is considered a giant oil field with 2 billion barrels of estimated reserves, this field had a peak production of 450 thousand barrels in 1999.

ANNEX IV

THE CONNECTION BETWEEN CRUDE OIL PRICES AND EXPLORATION

According to the U.S. Energy Information Administration (EIA, www.eia.gov) between 1949 and 2010 some 1,200 oil and natural gas exploration wells per year were spudded in the USA (including those targeting natural gas resources).

Extrapolating these numbers, we can estimate that in the last 100 years, some 120,000 exploration wells have been drilled in U.S. territory.

The same statistics reveal that between the years 1981 and 1984 the rate of drilling increased to an average of over 2,000 exploration holes per year (2,651 in 1981). Not surprisingly, a few years earlier, 1979 to 1981, oil had reached its' maximum historical price: 97.9 US$ in constant 2012 dollars (inflation adjusted), only surpassed by the average 2008 price of 98 US$, when prices hit 98.5 US$ in current dollars.

As we can see, in constant value, the price reached in 2008 is only ten cents above the 1980 price, and like nowadays, that "price peak" (sudden increase in prices) triggered an "exploration peak" that lasted from 1981 till 1984.

Not all oil wells are exploration wells

The reader will notice the large discrepancy between the numbers given (above 1,200 oil and gas exploration wells) and those shown in TABLE IX of PART D. In the latter we refer to the total number of drill holes for hydrocarbons that were spudded in the world in 2012. In that TABLE IX, for example, the total number of wells spudded inland in the U.S.A. were 47,918.

How does this fit in with the approximately 1,200 holes yearly indicated above?

The difference is that the 1,200 wells per year are strictly "oil exploration" drill holes, while the 47,918 include an enormous number of development or production wells, and includes both oil and natural gas ones. In fact, the U.S. is one of the few countries that keep records and statistics discriminating between exploration, development and production wells, while the majority of the countries just give the total number of wells drilled, with no distinction.

Even so, we can assume that the numbers valid for the U.S. can be valid for the rest of the world. Which means that if only 2.7% of the total number of wells drilled in the U.S.A. are considered exploration wells, the same percentage could be assumed for other nations, a mathematical exercise that churns out some hair-raising conclusions:

China = 670 exploration wells in a year, only one exploration well for every 5.600 sq m (slightly more than the surface of Lebanon, or about half the extension of Vermont).

Canada = 289 prospective drill-holes or one well every 13.336 sq m (about the surface of Switzerland).

Ex-U.S.S.R territories = 211 exploration wells per year. Only 211 drill-holes in a territory of 8.647.172 sq. mi.! An average of one well every 40,982 sq m (about the surface of Portugal).

Argentina, a sad 35 wells, and Mexico, a meager 32 exploration wells. The rest of the countries also show unbelievable trivial numbers: 19 in Venezuela and just 16 in Brazil.

It also hard to believe that only some 13 exploration wells per year will be drilled in Saudi Arabia.

Then, is there any possibility of considering that the world oil exploration IS NOT IN ITS' INFANCY?

THE TRUTH ABOUT "THE END OF CHEAP OIL"

TABLE XII displays the historical changes in oil prices indicated in constant dollars, i.e. taking into account the variation of the buying power of the dollar as time goes by as a result of inflation. After 1960, there are 5 clearly distinguishable periods in historical oil prices:

1 - The period before 1974 when oil was really cheap, or better, scandalously cheap, to the point where there was a surge in investigations and laboratory testing, experimenting on the possible profitable transformation of hydrocarbons into sugars and proteins for livestock feed; just the opposite to the present situation: manufacturing ethanol-derived fuels using corn or sugarcane.

2 - The period between 1974 and 1979, when the OPEC countries used a political event to suddenly multiply oil prices by five, starting an economic turmoil that immediately jeopardized the western economies, and setting off a series of stock market crashes and a general halt in economic development with worldwide effects, with the exception of the Persian Gulf states and other OPEC countries.

TABLE XII - OIL PRICES BETWEEN 1970 AND 2012

YEAR	REAL DOLLARS	2012 CONSTANT DOLLARS
1970	1.8	10.1
1971	3.6	20.7
1972	3.2	20.1
1973	3.3	16.1
1974	11.6	51.2
1975	11.5	43.7
1976	12.8	49.1
1978	14.0	46.9
1979	31.6	94.9
1980	36.8	97.9
1981	35.9	86.2
1982	33.0	74.5
1983	29.5	55.8
1985	27.6	55.8
1986	14.4	28.7
1987	18.4	35.4
1988	14.9	27.5
1989	18.2	32.1
1990	23.7	39.6
1991	20.0	32.0
1992	19.3	30.0
1993	17.0	25.6
1994	15.8	23.2
1996	20.7	28.7
1997	19.1	25.9
1998	12.7	17.0
1999	18.0	23.5
2000	28.5	36.1
2001	24.4	30.1
2003	28.8	34.2
2004	38.3	44.2
2005	54.5	60.9
2006	65.1	70.5
2007	72.4	76.1
2008	97.3	98.5
2009	61.7	62.7
2010	79.5	79.5
2011	96.1	95.8
2012	94.2	94.2

3 - A turbulent period between 1979 and 1982 in which prices showed wild fluctuations due to repeated episodes of tension between Middle East states and Israel, and contributing to bring about the historical maximum of 97.5 dollars (constant 2012 value in 1980).
4 - The period between 1982 and 2004, when prices progressively dropped approaching the dangerous pre-1974 rates. As a consequence of such low oil prices, most oil companies trashed all exploration budgets including vital investments for the development of new fields.
5 - The current period since 2004 'til present, with the unstoppable increase in oil prices, almost trebling the previous average, and including the historical 2008 maximum of 98.5 dollars, very close to the previous 1980 maximum.

As shown here, and following the arguments of many oil economics experts, it is pretty clear that crude oil prices are tightly related to issues of international politics (specially the periodical crises affecting the Persian Gulf and the Middle East countries in general) and have no ties with higher or lower oil reserves, production rates, "depletion" or "peaks" situations.

The data shown in TABLE XII de-mystifies the "end of cheap oil" legend since, as shown, oil prices barely moved away from the 40 to 70 dollars per barrel bracket, jumping to exceptional high prices in the period between 1979 and 1982, due to political issues and still above the averages of the 2006 to 2012 interlude. Even today, it is not clear that recent oil prices are higher than in previous years (unless we compare to those before 1974). The average price in 2008 was the same as that of 1980, and the low average price in 1998 is quite similar to that of 1973.

ANNEX V

THE ANCIENT MEDICINAL USE OF OIL, MUD VOLCANOES AND CHIMAERAS

According to a local tradition, towards the end of the Middle Ages, the monks from the Benedictine Tegernsee Abbey sold the oil that oozed from rocks next to the Saint Quirinus chappel as "the miraculous Oil of Saint Quirinus", with numerous healing properties, both real and illusory. It must have some sort of effect, since even today, the locals and visitors from afar still flock to the natural oil spring to fill their containers with this "miraculous oil". The Saint Quirinus oil spring is close to the western shore of the Tegernsee Lake, not far to the city of Bad Wiessee, in Bavaria, some 30 miles South of Munich. After 1881, several entrepreneurs sunk a number of prospective wells in the area, many being "dusters", except for one that achieved a puny total production of about 1,500 barrels of oil. Years later, the region was drilled by Shell, and between 1906 and 1919, a total of 30,000 barrels were tapped.

This story is similar to the so-called "Thyrsus' Blood", a legend about the blood of a giant towards the end the Roman colonization of the Tyrolean Alps, in the Seefeld region, some 12 miles northeast of Innsbruck, Austria. Once again, the "blood" is nothing but mineral oil contained in bituminous shales. As very little oil was oozing from the rock, the locals used to heat the shales to obtain a few drops of the precious concoction. By the end of the 19th century some smart industrialists started a number of mechanized distillation business, this time not looking for the "miraculous blood" but rather to the profit obtained by selling kerosene for lamps. Soon, numerous quarries were opening in the region, creating new jobs and wealth for the locals but, alas, spoiling the beautiful, natural scenery of this alpine area. Fortunately the quarries had to be closed and abandoned, since distillation couldn't compete with much cheaper oil imported from the U.S.A. (Pennsylvania) and Russia (Baku).

In 1694, Pierre Pomet, a famous Parisian pharmacist, published a manual on pharmacy which became very popular at the time. In his book, he reported on the soothing properties of a mineral oil that was gathered on the banks of a creek near the town of Gabian, some 12 miles North of the city of Béziers, in the Languedoc province. The oil seep was locally known as "Font de l'oli", in those days an exclusive property of the bishopric of Béziers, who administered and commercialized its' product. By then, the spring used to leak some 18 pints per day, but towards the end of the 17th century the fluid had dwindled down to a mere 2 pints per day. Of course, the healing properties of this oil were well-known amongst the Christianity of southern France, although not as famous as its' equivalent, the Italian "Olio di Modena". Surprisingly, nothing more was heard about the Gabian spring after the 17th century and no records were kept on the results of two wells bored in the area in 1885. Even so, the legend was convincing enough to call prospective entrepreneurs to the area, resulting in several successful oil-producing wells there and elsewhere in the neighboring southern Pyrenees.

Another asphalt spring associated to bituminous rocks in a different French region was also known since the Middle Ages. It was called Pechelbronn (bitumen springs in German), on the left bank of the Rhine River, some 34 miles North of Strasbourg. During the 18th century, as elsewhere, the asphalt sands were firstly hand-mined and distilled. The first conventional mine pits and galleries were sunk towards 1850, and, finally, the first mechanical well drilling, in 1878. Nowadays, no oil is tapped from Pechelbronn, but ironically, a few miles from the old wells, the installations of a modern geothermal project called Soultz-sous-Forêt was sited. It is the largest European experiment that tries to make use of the geothermal heat from dry rocks (a method different to the ones employed to obtain geothermal energy in volcanic sites like Iceland or Italy). Enhanced Geothermal Energy is probably the biggest potential alternative energy source for the planet, and the only method that allows a constant and uniform generation of electricity 24/365, with practically no environmental impact. Most probably, the one that will definitively replace oil as a source of energy.

None of the "medical mineral oil" seeps already mentioned attain the "Hall of Fame" status like the oil springs of "Olio di Modena" did. The petroleum trickling from that location in Italy was mentioned in 1462 as a famous cure for leprosy (probably really ringworm or scabbies). Not surprisingly, there are still numerous examples of "mud volcanoes" in this Italian region, and some of them can still be visited at the Natural Reserve of Salse di Nirano, 2.5 miles southeast of Sassuolo (10 miles South of Modena) and at Salsa di Regnano, 10.6 miles West of Sassuolo, both in the Parma region. In Sicily, too, the mud volcanoes of the Natural Reserve of Maccalube di Aragona, about 9 miles North of Agrigento, were famous for their healing properties, as were those at Maccalube di Caltanissetta, some 25 miles to the northeast of Agrigento. Even though the morphological and functional characteristics of the Sicilian mud volcanoes are the same as the ones in Modena, they don't have visible hydrocarbons in their composition, being only salt water and methane gas. Of course, both the Modena and Agrigento regions have been thoroughly prospected for oil since the end of the 19th century, and several oil and gas deposits have been located that produced millions of barrels; even today, the Sicilian offshore has an interesting potential. The first wells drilled in the Parma region were started in 1892 by a French company, later bought by the Societá Petroli d'Italia, followed by the discovery of the Montechiaro and Ozzano fields in a region located to the West of Modena (Parma). In 1923, the main Salsomaggiore field was discovered, resulting in the founding cornerstone of AGIP (Azienda Generale Italiana Petroli). This last company has also discovered several small oil and gas fields in the South of Sicily, not too far from already mentioned ancient "maccalube", or mud volcanoes.

Although discovered in 1989, the Tempa Rossa oilfield wasn't developed until very recently. This field is located in southern Italy, midway between the town of Potenza and the Gulf of Tarento. Tempa Rossa is operated by the French company Total, which hopes to start production in early 2016, with a yield of 50,000 bbld of crude plus 1,700 bbld of condensates and 8 million cf/day of natural gas. The oilfield contains 200 million bbl of measured oil reserves. It is an outstanding example of potential oilfields that can still be found in Europe, in spite of more than a century of exploration and drilling.

Mud volcanoes are small hills or cones formed by the spewing of clayish mud in a salt-water suspension, together with hydrocarbons and methane, formed deep in the Earth's crust, and in the majority of the cases, related with the presence of hydrocarbon-rich sediments below. Those hydrocarbon gases and liquids reach the surface channeled by some type of tectonic fracture or fault (many are activated, or de-activated by an earthquake in the region).
The most famous mud volcanoes are those located at Baku in Azerbaijan (on the shores of the Caspian Sea and associated with the still more famous oil fields), or the ones situated at the eastern end of the Crimean Peninsula. But the most spectacular ones are those found in Balochistan (Pakistan) with several of them attaining over 650 ft in height, the largest of which is 1,550 ft high. As well as being artisanal oil springs, these mud volcanoes are usually rich in methane gas, which can burn accidentally, causing the

extraordinary and rare cases of "chimaeras" with magical or religious connotations.

Juan Rodríguez Cabrillo, explorer of the Californian coast, was the first westerner who, in 1542, saw "a sea of oil" in the Santa Barbara Bay, in Goleta, California. Following the local natives' example, he also made the best of the tar to re-caulk his flag ship, the San Salvador. In fact, the accumulations of tar are so frequent in the area that, in later years, one of the beaches became known as "Punta Carbon" (Coal Oil Point). The studies carried out by the University of California - Santa Barbara (its' campus is in Goleta) calculate that the sea bed at Goleta oozes out some 250 barrels of oil per day, from some 2,000 different seep-points.

CHIMAERAS

Undoubtedly the most famous chimaera or natural flaming fire is the group of a dozen flaring vents located at the slopes of the Yanartas (flaming rock) valley in the Antalya Province in southwestern Turkey (near the town of Ciraly). Apart from being a stunning view, the main reason for their fame is the fact that these natural fires have been burning for the last 2,500 years, at least since the days of Ctesias of Cnidus, a Greek physician and historian of the 5th century BC. Today this famous locality is often visited by European tourists that enjoy the nearby Antalya beaches on the Mediterranean.

But those Americans that are not very fond of jet flying can find a similar phenomenon closer to home:
- The permanent burning fire located in Chestnut Ridge Park, New York.
- The chimaera found in Cook Forest State Park in northwestern Pennsylvania.

This burning methane seeps are different from more common gas seeps associated to oil deposits and mud volcanoes as described above. One of the most striking differences is that dry methane seeps from fissures in solid crystalline rock with no sediments or fluids associated. Giuseppe Etiope, is a notorious researcher at the National Institute of Geophysics and Volcanology in Italy and a world expert on natural gas seeps and eternal flames. After studying several chimaeras around the world he is convinced that since they don't result from organic matter decay, they must be related to chemical reactions at depth. Since most are associated to ultrabasic rock layers it is assumed that methane is generated by a reaction involving water and CO_2. The gas is therefore of "abiogenic" origin, that is unrelated to organic, biological residues, although some recent chemical analysis of the burning gas in Yanartas showed that a fraction of the 87% methane has an organic origin.

CONCLUSIONS

Abridging all the above issues, we can draw the following conclusions:

1. King Hubbert's first mistake: the historical production of an oil field can be represented as a "Gaussian Bell distribution" curve
This is the main argument that doomsayers put forth to decide whether a given oil field is in a depletion phase or close to reaching it, or past its' "peak production" (Peak Oil Theory). It means that if we analyze the historical production of an oil field from the start, yield figures will follow a bell-shaped curve with a "peak" of maximum production from where it will decline year after year, drawing a diminishing curve that will be approximately symmetrical to the production rate increase. This means that one can predict the depletion rate of the oil field and forecast volume withdrawals and years left before the field becomes a "duster".
Fortunately that is not the case, and if the historical production curves of oil fields around the world are analyzed, a curve very similar to the one shown in FIGURE 1 will be obtained. That is, a "mesa" or "plateau" instead of a "peak", which is followed by more "plateaus" that result from artificial raises, and later, from EOR methods. Every time that an EOR is implemented on the field, yields are increased, so that in the end the falling half of the production decline shows a much less steep angle than the one produced by the "peak oil" theory.

2. The unconceivable second error of King Hubbert: to apply a theory designed for an oil field to an entire country.
The "Gaussian Bell Curve" of an oilfield cannot be extended to several, or most of, the producing wells of a country. Each oilfield has its own production history based on the geology of the deposit and the technical innovations that were available at the time of its exploitation. Although Hubbert very successfully predicted the "peak oil" volume of 9,637,000 bbl/day in the 48 lower states for 1970, it becomes clearer as years pass that the fall in production is quite asymmetrical to the historic build-up. On analyzing FIGURE 4 a flattening tendency after a broad plateau during the 1970-1990 lapse, is clearly seen, with a resistance to depletion in the 5 to 6

million bbl/day interval.

Assuming a symmetrical Bell Curve, the 1930 oil production of 2,460,000 bbl/day should have been equal to the 2010 production, 40 years after de 1970 "peak", but unfortunately for the "Peak Oil Theory" supporters, the 2010 more than DOUBLED to 5,474,000 bbl/d.

It must be stressed that all the figures given in this analysis refer to "conventional oil" and excluding the production from Alaska, the Gulf of Mexico offshore, oil shales or condensates. The total production figure for the USA was 7,513,000 bbl/d in 2010 if all oil fields yields are considered.

FIGURE 4

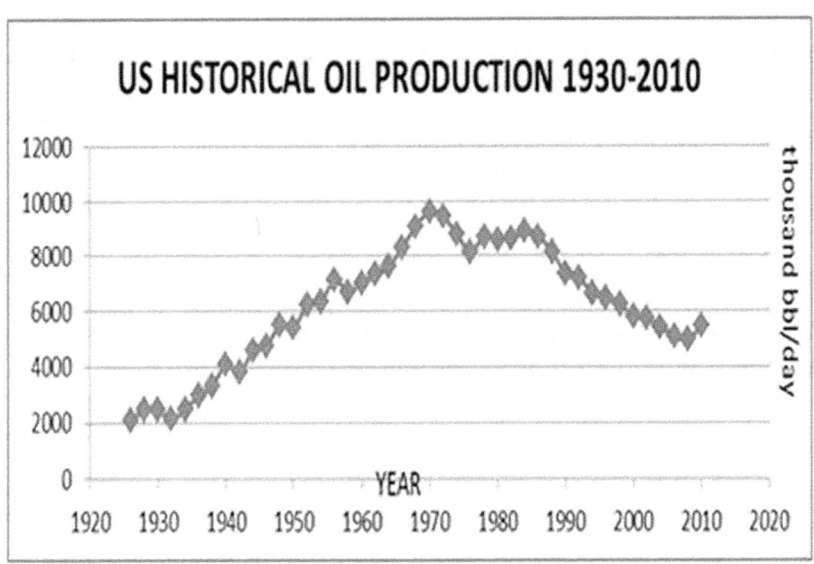

3. The doomsayers were always wrong and persist in their errors without dismay

From the first days of oil exploration, several alarmists started their gloomy announcements of coming oil depletion. At the twilight of the 20th century, and based on King Hubbert's hypothesis, the naysayers cried that the known oil fields' production would be insufficient to cover the demand, and that no new oilfields were found after a thorough prospection. They were proved wrong; year after year they deceived their followers.

Very recently they change their strategy and now claim that although there will be no ultimate depletion, the oil prices would escalate to unmatched levels, making gasoline a fuel only available to the rich.

4. The "end of cheap oil" is a false myth

As it is shown in TABLE XII the oil prices in constant dollars (adjusted for inflation) based on the current price of oil in 2010 reached a high value of 98.5 US$/barrel but then decreased to 62.7 US$ in 2009 and 79.5 US$ in 2010. As can be noted, the 2008 oil price was similar to the 1980 price of 97.5 US$/barrel.

5. The doomsayers ignore the modern EOR techniques

Conventional oil pumping remained almost unchanged for a century and only allowed for the recovery of an average 30% of the oil "in situ", with rear and exceptional cases of higher recoveries. Today, several systems of Enhanced Oil Recovery techniques allow for withdrawals of nearly 60% of the oil stocked in the reservoir rocks. Some of these techniques are costly and can only be implemented in periods of high oil prices.. Some oil companies prefer to invest in depleted oil-fields that have still a working and reliable infrastructure than to venture into risky and remote targets, sometimes plagued with political uncertainties. Some experts believe that a 10% yield increase in an old field is much better than investment in risky lands.

6. The doomsayers wrongly state that the whole planet has been thoroughly prospected and there are very limited possibilities of increasing the world oil reserves

This is so obviously false that no effort is necessary to demonstrate that the true is quite the opposite.

Just consider the argument that in the last 75 years most of the exploration effort was concentrated in the U.S. and a few other, selected areas of the world, while many extensive countries well-endowed with known, large and thick sedimentary deposits remain un-prospected. In many countries in Africa or South America only a dozen exploration wells were spudded over vast basins, most of the times being relatively shallow, while extensive marine platforms remain virtually unexplored.

Take the case of Mali, in Africa, where only one exploration hole was sunk for every 450.000 sq. mi. of territory.

WORLD OIL EXPLORATION IS, FOR MOST OF THE PLANET, IN ITS INFANCY AND PLENTY OF HYDROCARBON RESOURCES ARE WAITING TO BE BROUGHT TO LIGHT.

Prof. J.C. Mirre

ABOUT THE AUTHOR

Juan Carlos Mirre is a geologist graduated from the Universidad de Buenos Aires (Argentina) with a MSc degree and a Masters in Economic Geology from the Sorbonne University (Paris, France). During his professional life he was in charge of numerous projects as an exploration geologist in many countries in South America, Europe and Western Asia. He was also involved in a number of studies concerning the environmental impact assessment of development and operation projects. He is also an author of both scientific papers and science for general audience articles and books, mostly written in Spanish. The author is also a Private tutor for Masters and graduate degrees in Economic & Applied Geology.

www.ingramcontent.com/pod-product-compliance
Lightning Source LLC
Chambersburg PA
CBHW051336170526
45166CB00002B/838